SKETCH

OF

CORNISH GRAMMAR.

BY

EDWIN NORRIS.

OXFORD:
AT THE UNIVERSITY PRESS.
M.DCCC.LIX.

TABLE OF CONTENTS.

LETTERS	3
ARTICLES	12
SUBSTANTIVES	12
ADJECTIVES	22
NUMBERS	23
PRONOUNS	26
VERBS	41
IRREGULARS	66
ADVERBS	73
PREPOSITIONS	80
CONJUNCTIONS	86
CONSTRUCTION	89

INTRODUCTORY NOTE.

The following Grammatical Sketch of the Cornish language is made up of the observations jotted down by the Compiler, whilst engaged in preparing a translation of the three ancient Cornish Dramas entitled Ordinalia, contained in a Manuscript belonging to the Bodleian Library. After a considerable portion of that work was printed off, he was induced to arrange his notes in some order, for the purpose of adding them to the book as an appendix, and by doing this he found himself empowered to see further into the structure of the language than he anticipated, and to understand many passages which he had left as unintelligible; he discovered regularity in many cases where he had supposed that all was disorder, and found that much of the apparent confusion arose from the entire absence of any system of orthography.

From the way in which this essay was compiled, it is obvious that all illustrations of rules given in it are drawn from the work alluded to, except only in the very few cases where the Mount Calvary has furnished data for completing the evidence which the Ordinalia would have left imperfect. It is also a consequence of this way of proceeding that a form or a construction of frequent occurrence is often elucidated by a single example, while a rarer case will be furnished with several instances in proof, perhaps all that the compiler could find; in the former case there could be no reason for hesitation, and consequently no motive for accumulating evidence; in the latter, infrequency produced doubt, which could not be removed without collating all the cases in point.

It is necessary to bear in mind that, during the whole work of translation, the process was tentative. The translator fully acknowledges the valuable aid he has received from the grammar of Lhuyd and the vocabulary compiled by Tonkin, which appeared under the name of Pryce; without them he could have done nothing; but he must say that his suspicion of the accuracy of these aids, of the vocabulary especially, was continually on the increase; and that until he had found a word justified by frequent repetition and obvious congruity, he never felt confident in the value affixed to it, unless it were corroborated by Welsh or Armoric analogy.

The Grammar was more satisfactory, but it was chiefly based on the practice of Cornish as spoken in Lhuyd's day, a dialect which had lost much of the character of the old language in which the best monuments were written; it was also slightly modified by the habit of the author, who unconsciously deviated now and then into the forms of his native Welsh.

After these observations, the compiler believes he may offer this Essay as a useful help to a reader of Cornish; he is quite conscious that it is incomplete, but he trusts that what is included in it will not be found inaccurate.

SKETCH OF CORNISH GRAMMAR.

§. 1. LETTERS.

The orthography of the manuscripts is so irregular, that it is quite impracticable, in a grammatical essay, to follow it into all its varieties; we find every word of any length written in half a dozen forms, such as *diuath, deweth, dyweth, devyth, dyvyth, diweth,* &c. &c.; and so short a word as *kig* is found under the forms of *kyg, kyc, kic, cyk,* and probably more. It appears advisable in this sketch to keep to one form only, and the one selected will be that which most commonly occurs; if this be doubtful, then the form most analogous to the Welsh or Breton. The writer of the Dramas was guided merely by his ear, which was variable, and in addition to this, he was undecided whether he should follow the English or Welsh sounds of the letters. Very frequently too the handwriting is uncertain; and nothing but a knowledge of the language will enable a reader to distinguish between *c* and *t, u* and *n, b* and *v,* and some others.

For this reason it seems most expedient first to give a list of the sounds of the language, and then to shew how they are expressed in the manuscripts; to adopt, as above stated, one form only, but in quotations, to follow the original spelling in all its variety.

§. 2. *Vowels.*

The vowel sounds were *a, e, i, o, u,* and *aw.* The last was like our *a* in 'all,' a sound hardly known in most European tongues; the others as in Italian.

A, as in 'father,' is always made by *a* in the MS. *E*, as in 'there,' always by *e*. *I*, as our *ee*, is generally written *y*, rarely *i*, and now and then *e*, especially in the pronoun *my*, which is often written *me*, no doubt from the influence of English orthography; in this grammar *y* is used. *O* and *u* are generally so written. *Aw* is, I think, always written *o*.

Lhuyd, who wrote when the language was spoken, adopted *a* turned upside down to express the sound of *aw*; he thus wrote *mɐz* where we find *mos*. We have *hos*, O 132, "a duck," which he would have written *hɐz*; it is *hoet* in the ancient vocabulary, and those who spelled the word by ear wrote *hawz*; see Pryce, voc. *hoet*. It does not appear that *aw* and *o* were etymologically distinguished, any more than the vowels in the English words *fall* and *hot*; and as in the majority of cases it would now be difficult to decide which sound was used, no attempt is made here to represent it by a distinct character.

§. 3. The vowels are liable to a modification which the Germans, after Grimm, call "umlaut;" a change which brings the different syllables of a word into harmony with each other. It is defined as an inflection of *a*, *o*, and *u*, in the radical syllable of a word, caused by the influence or attraction of an *i* or *u* in a subsequent servile syllable expressed or understood; *a* becoming *e*, *o* becoming *ö*, (the French *eu*) and *u* becoming *ü* (the French *u*). It is such an influence which makes *feci* out of *facio* in Latin, and *feet*, *men*, and *elder*, out of *foot*, *man*, *old*, in English. In Cornish this law was strictly observed, though the unsettled orthography produced much irregularity in its expression. I think the following rule will conveniently shew its practical operation:—whenever a word with *a* or *e* for its final vowel (and sometimes the influence reaches a preceding vowel) receives by grammatical change the addition of a syllable whose vowel is *i* (*y*) or *eu*, the *a* becomes *e* or *y*, and the *e* becomes *y*: thus from *car*, "to love," is made *kyrys*, "loved," R 892, and *kyrreugh*, "ye love," O 543; from *taw*, "to be silent," comes *teweugh*, "be ye silent," R 669, and *tywyn*, "we are silent," R 2527: from *gwel*, "to see," *gwylsyn*, "we saw," R 807: from *guas*, "a lad," *guesyon*, "lads," D 1299. The letter *e*, in fact, is neutral, and may stand either for *a* or *y*: thus we find *kerry*, D 2240, *kyrry*, O 537, or *kyry*, D 1289, "thou mayest love;" *lavaraf*, O 7, or *levaraf*, O 1653, "I say." Even English words receive the same modifications; as from *handle*, D 3194, we have *hyndlyf*, R 1531. *O* and *u* sometimes remain unaltered, but are more commonly changed to *e;* as from *danfon*, "to send," *danfeneugh*, "send," R 1594; from *torr*, "to break," *der*[a], "will break," O 2184; from *cous*, "to speak," *keus*, "speaks," D 1676; from *curene*, "to crown," D 2064, we find *kerenys*, O 2381, *kerunys*, O 2391, and *kurenys* in a variant reading of O 2374; the difficulty of distinguishing *e* from *o* in the manuscript will not let me cite *koroneugh* of O 2347 as a still further change; *arluth*, "lord," makes in the plural *arlythy*, D 1900.

A termination in *a* does not change a root with a vowel *y;* from *pys*, "to pray," we have *pysaf*, "I pray," O 1390; but *losco* from *lesky* occurs in R 130-

---

[a] In some former state of the language this form must have had a final *i;* it still remains in the Irish verb.

§. 4. *Consonants.*

The consonantal sounds are *b, d, th* (as in 'the'), *f, g* hard, *g* soft, *h, k, l, m, n, p, r, s, sh, ch, t, th* (as in 'think'), *v, w, wh, z*. Of these sounds *b, d, f, h, l, m, n, p, r, s, t*, are written in the MSS. regularly with the letters above given.

Th, as in the English 'the,' is always so written in the manuscript of the Ordinalia. It is the aspirate form of *d*, and in Welsh is made by *dd;* in the British Museum MS. of Mount Calvary, and in the Bodleian MS. of the Creation, written in 1611, it is made by a character not unlike ȝ; those who wrote Cornish in its last days represented the sound by *dh*, and in the very ancient Cornish vocabulary the same combination is used; for example, in the word *medhec*, "a physician." The Armoric equivalent is *z*. I would have written *dh* in this grammar, if I had always been sure of distinguishing the two sounds of *th*, but as this is not the case, I write *ṭh;* a mistake seems of less consequence when indicated by a mere dot; and moreover this form is a smaller departure from the orthography of the Ordinalia. But I have no doubt that I have often omitted the dot when it ought to be inserted.

G, as in 'gold,' is so written in the MSS. Lhuyd used the Saxon ȝ to distinguish this sound from the following. It is now and then irregularly employed as an initial instead of *d*, as in *geyṭh*, "a day," O 39, instead of *dyṭh*, O 49.

G soft, as in 'gentle,' is not a genuine Cornish letter, but a simple corruption of *s;* we thus find *pygy*, "to pray," and *gage*, "to leave," instead of *pysy* and *gase*. It is like the vulgarism of *squeege* for *squeeze*. Lhuyd sometimes used *dzh* for this sound, a clumsy but accurate representation. I have no occasion to mention the sound in this essay.

H is etymologically equivalent to the Welsh *ch*; it is the aspirate form of *k*. *Colon*, "heart," becomes *holon*, O 2135, and *cowethes*, "a companion," becomes *howethes*, O 113. When final, it is almost always made by *gh*, as in *levereugh*, "you say," D 781, the Welsh *lafarwch*.

K is made in the MSS., as in English, by *c* before consonants and *a*, *o*, and *u*, and by *k* before *e*, *i*, and *y*. Thus *car*, "he loves," *caradow*, "beloved," O 1114, *kerry*, "thou lovest," O 2142; *cref*, "strong," D 2539, O 2222. Now and then we find irregularities in this usage; as in *cemeres* for *kemeres*, O 1123; *krev* for *cref*, O 687; *cen* for *ken*, D 1994.

There appears to be a trace of the Welsh aspirate *ll*, if I am right in supposing *Behethlen*, O 2588, to be *Bohellan*; to this I was led by the equivalent *Beheath-land*, given in Pryce's list of Cornish villages; *thl* might be an attempt to represent the peculiar sound of the Welsh *ll*.

No trace appears of the curious change of *m* and *n* to *bm* and *dn*, the latter of which is so common in names of places in Cornwall, and in the more recent MS. of the 'Creation.' It must have crept in between 1450 and 1600, though it may have existed in speaking at an earlier date.

The sound of *s* was probably like that of the English *s*, varying to that of *z* when between vowels, as in 'rose.' It is this last sound which I suppose to be occasionally corrupted to *g*, as mentioned before. *Sh* occurs in English words only, and is written *sch* or *sh*; see *sheft*, O 2494, *schapys*, O 2562.

Th, as in 'think,' is always so written in this Grammar; it is the aspirate form of *t*, as *ṯh* is of *d*. The frequent use of *th* instead of *s* shews that the sound was not so definite as in English; we have *grath*, O 6, instead of *gras*, "grace; *fath* for the English *face*, O 1412; *cowys*, R 405, and *cowyth*, R 410; *sacrifyth*, O 1519, and *sacryfys*, O 1493. In *Natharet*, D 301, for *Nazareth*, the *ṯh* is probably intended. The equivalent sound has become a pure sibilant in Armoric, and is written *z*.

Ch is an English sound, and is used in words borrowed from English, as *chacys*, "chased," O 706; *cherite*, "charity," O 1782; *cher*, "cheer," D 1824; *chyf*, "chief," O 2331. The sound must have occurred in one genuine Celtic word *chy*, "a house," which is written with a *t* in all other Celtic languages. *Ty* is found in the ancient vocabulary, but I think *chy* everywhere else. In D 334, if *ow thy* be the true reading, we have a genuine case of *ty* with the proper mutation; but the difficulty of distinguishing *c* from *t* renders it uncertain. *Ch* frequently occurs in the ancient vocabulary where *k* is intended.

The sound of *v* is generally represented by that letter, but it is also found not unfrequently expressed by *f*, as in Welsh; unmistakeable instances of this are *fenygough*, "ye bless," D 2646; *fynnaf*, "I will," D 2496; *yn fras*, "greatly," R 1098.

W appears to have had the English sound; it is not unfrequently confounded with *u*, particularly after *g*.

Wh represents the Welsh *chw*, but it is often confounded with *w*; as in *whylly*, D 2101, *wylly*, O 745, "thou mayest see."

The consonantal sound of *y* is made usually by *i*, and sometimes by a character frequently read *z*, but certainly sounded *y*. We have such a character in old English MSS., where we find *zoung*, *zear*, *zou*; it is often so printed in transcripts, but the propriety of so transcribing is doubtful.

Z is not written, but is represented by *s*, as mentioned before. In one case alone have I found it, O 2358; see the note on that line.

§. 5. *Mutations of Consonants.*

In all the Celtic languages, many of the consonants at the beginning of a word suffer changes according to fixed rules, under certain grammatical or euphonic conditions. In most of these changes the Cornish coincides with the Welsh, in a few it is more like the Armoric; the fourth form, or nasal change of the Welsh, is unknown. The surds *p*, *k*, and *t*, have each two mutations, or three forms; the sonants *b*, *g*, and *d* have one mutation, or two forms[a]; *m* has the same change as *b*. The other letters are not subject to change.

The writers on Welsh grammar have given various names to these several forms: what one writer calls the soft form another calls light; the same is named aspirate by one and nasal by the other. I therefore propose to call the radical letter the first, and the two mutations, the second and the third forms, as all are agreed upon the order in which they come. When I wish to designate the form which ought to follow any given word, I shall occa-

---

[a] The sonants have a second mutation, which will be noticed presently; but it is a return to the surd form, and is not of the nature of the other changes. I would call it negative.

sionally put a little numeral over the word by way of abbreviation; writing for example ow^3, "my," and y^2, "his," to shew that the initial consonant of the words following these possessive pronouns must take the respective forms which the figures point out.

The changes of the surd letters are precisely those of the so-called tenues to mediæ and aspiratæ in Greek grammar; as π, β, φ, &c. In Cornish these are $p, b, f; k, g, h; t, d, th$. In the sonant letters the one change is to what we may call the aspirate sonant: b becomes v (bh), d becomes th (dh), and g might have been, by analogy, made gh, with a guttural sound, perhaps like that of the Greek digamma; but as gh was already employed for the aspirate of c when final, and as moreover the aspirate gh has in most languages shewn a tendency to disappear, the g in this state is either left out altogether, or changed to w, and more rarely to wh, as in D 2156. In the same instances the Welsh omits the g, and the Bretons write $c'h$, unless a w follow the g, in which case g is omitted, as in Welsh. M, like b, becomes v. In the sonant letters the third form is like the first.

In accordance with the above described mutations, we may form the following table:—

1	2	3
P	B	F
K	G	H
T	D	Th
B	V	B
G	W, or nothing	G
D	Th	D
M	V	M

The cases of mutation will appear in the grammar, but a few examples are here given:—

MUTATION OF CONSONANTS. 11

Ou³ fehas (pehas), "my sins," O 2257; *y² das (tas),* "his father," O 2740; *y² vam (mam),* "his mother," O 2740; *aga³ threys (treys),* "their feet," O 760; *ou³ banneth,* "my blessing," O 2168; *y² volnogeth (bolnogeth),* "his will," O 2352; *the² wovyn (govyn),* "to ask," D 2667; *the ase (gase),* "to leave," D 2035. Once I find *ch* changed to *g: the gy (chy),* "thy house," O 1018.

The sonants *b, g, d,* are also subject to take the surd forms of *p, k, t;* this initial mutation is unknown to the Welsh tongue, but it is found in Armoric; Zeuss has named it provection. I mark the words with ° which produce this change. Examples are, *ow querthe (guerthe),* "selling," D 1520; *a pe (be),* "if it were," R 1662; *ou tos (dos),* "coming," O 1651; *mar kruge (gruge),* "if I do," D 875; *yn ta (da),* "well," D 1905. We have the singular form *ou fysky (guysky),* "striking," O 1685.

In Cornish, as in Welsh and Armoric, the *f* suffers no change. It seems however that in the latest days of the existence of the language, a mutation was made like that of *b* and *m*. Lhuyd mentions *an vordh,* "the way," from *forth,* p. 241, as well as a more peculiar change to *h* in the oblique case, as *a'n hlôh,* "of the child," from *flôh,* p. 242. I have not seen a trace of such mutations in the manuscript.

In the Armoric, *s* is regularly changed to *z*. I have found only one case of the change; it occurs in O 2358.

Observe generally that the mutations are often neglected in the manuscripts, and nothing must be concluded from their absence. This is also the case with ancient Welsh, Breton, and Irish writings, though the practice is now to insert them regularly in every instance. It is most probable that they were always used in speaking, however the writer may have neglected to spell in accordance with the pronunciation.

§. 6. ARTICLES.

The definite Article is *an* (*en*) for all numbers and genders; as, *an myghtern*, "the king," R 104; *an venen*, "the woman," D 516; *an porthow*, "the gates," R 98. When it is in connection with a preceding word ending with a vowel, the article usually loses its own vowel, and the *n* is added to the preceding word. In this work the *n* is divided by an apostrophe, which is not found in the manuscripts.

The article has no inflection, but the cases are made by prepositions: as *en tas ha'n map ha'n spyrys*, "the Father and the Son and the Spirit," O 4: *an mor ha'n tyryow*, "the sea and the lands," O 26: *the'n tas*, "to the Father," D 626: *a'n nef*, "from the heaven," O 1319: *war an kunys*, "upon the wood," O 1333: *the'n dor*, "to the ground," O 1448.

The indefinite article is *un* for both genders; it is rarely used. Ex. *un map*, "a son," O 639; *worth un venen*, "to a woman," O 419.

§. 7. SUBSTANTIVES.

In Cornish, as in the other Celtic languages, a substantive is either masculine or feminine: the chief, though not the only grammatical distinction, between masculine and feminine, is the change of an initial consonant, when mutable, to one of the second class, in a feminine substantive of the singular number. Examples are: *un venen (benen),* "a woman," O 419; *an venen,* D 516; *an dre (tre),* "the town," O 2282; *an wethen (gwethen),* "the tree," O 201; *an bous (pous),* "the robe," R 1921-4. The same change distinguishes the gender of an adjective used substantively; as, *an casadow,* m. O 2119; *an gasadow,* f. O 2691, "the hated person."

Males and females have sometimes names of different origin, as *den,* "a man," *benen,* "a woman;" in many cases the name of the female differs from that of the male by the addition of *es;* as *arluth,* "lord," D 1957, *arlothes,* "lady," D 1965; *pystryor,* "a wizard," D 1767, *pestryores,* "a witch," O 2668; *cowyth,* "a male companion," O 2043, *cowethes,* "a female companion," O 92; *maw,* "a boy," D 1794, *mowes,* "a girl," D 1876.

§. 8. *Plural.*

The plural number has many forms; one of the commonest ends in *ow:* the Welsh *au,* Breton *ou.* A few examples follow:—

tassow, fathers,	O 1409	from	*tas,* O 1.
dornow, hands,	D 1390	..	*dorn,* R 2178.
roow, gifts,	O 2314, 2598	..	*ro,* O 2467.
fosow, walls,	O 2320	..	*fos,* O 2281.
scovornow, ears,	D 1361	..	*scoforn,* D 1144.
kentrow, nails,	D 2698	..	*kenter,* D 2676.
dewow, gods,	O 2692	..	*deu,* O 2564.
lyfryow, books,	D 78, 101	..	*levyr,* D 1157.
enevow, souls,	D 144	..	*enef,* D 1753.
trevow, towns,	D 132	..	*tre* (Welsh, *tref.*)
tyryow, lands	O 26	..	*tyr,* D 392.

14   CORNISH GRAMMAR.

A very common termination for plurals of personal words is *ion:* Welsh *ion,* Breton *ien.* These generally change the final vowel:—

> *Mebyon,* sons,   O 1038 from *map,* R 933.
> *guesyon,* fellows,   D 1299 .. *guas,* R 1824.
> *yethewon,* Jews,   D 2013 .. *yethow,* D 2003.
> *marregyon,* knights, D 1613 ⎫
> *marrouggyon,* do.   O 1639 ⎭ .. *marrek,* O 2139.

Some adjectives used as substantives take the same form:—

> *kefyon,* wise persons, D 1026 ⎫ from *cuf,* O 395.
> *cufyon,* .... D 1075 ⎭
> *gueryon,* true men, D 1305   from *guyr,* R 977.

Also some common nouns:—

> *prevyon,* reptiles,   O 1160.
> *govegyon,* sorrows, D 1062.
> *empynyon,* brains,   D 2120.
> *marthogyon,* wonders, O 2546.

We have also *laddron,* "thieves," D 2255, from *lader,* D 1174.

Many plurals end in *y:* this form is also found in Welsh and Armoric, but not so frequently:—

> *ysyly,* limbs,   D 1733.
> *esely* ..   O 2735.
> *mowysy,* maids,   D 944.   *mowes,* D 1876.
> *anfugy,* sins?   D 1473. *anfus,* D 1501.
> *profugy,* prophets, D 1480. *profus,* D 1465.
> *servysy,* servants, O 235.
> *guythysy,* guards, O 2038.
> *arlythy,* lords   D 1900. *arluth,* D 393.
> *mestrygy,* masters D 1711. ⎫ *mester* D 1736.
> *mestrigi,* ..   D 1647. ⎭

In some words the plural is the stem, and the singular adds the syllable *en,* which is here an individualizing particle.

SUBSTANTIVES. 15

delen, a leaf, *deyl*, leaves, O 254; also *dylyow*, O 777.
gryghonen, a spark, D 2717, *guryghon*, sparks, D 2101.
guelen, a rod, O 1444, *gueel*, rods, O 1957.
guethen, a tree, O 186, *gueyth*, trees, O 28.
luhesen, a flash of lightning, R 293, *luhes*, lightnings, R 296.

In Armoric, nouns denoting the condition of men, as well as names of animals, form their plural by adding *ed*. In Cornish the *d* has become *s* as usual, and more rarely *th*:—

eleth, angels,   R 190 from *el*, R 787.
myrhes, daughters,   O 1038 ⎫
myrghes,   D 2639 ⎭ .. *myrgh*, O 2736.
benenes, women,   O 2247 .. *benen*, O 256.
flehes, children,   O 1036 ⎫
flehas, O 1031; *fleghas*, D 1924 ⎭ .. *flogh*, O 806.
abesteleth, apostles,   R 893.
bredereth, brethren,   D 714 ⎫
brudereth, ...   D 1430 ⎭ .. *broder*, O 525.
puskes, fishes,   O 43 .. *pysk*, O 139.
bestes, beasts,   O 312 .. *best*, O 798.
syllyes, eels,   O 136.

Many words have plurals formed by a change of vowel only; this is evidently the *umlaut*, the Cornish application of which is described in §. 3. Thus we have

trys, D 835, *treys*, D 2937, feet, from *trous*, D 860, *tros*, D 2781.
meyn, stones,   D 62 from *men*, D 3211.
breder, brothers, R 1163 .. *broder*, O 525.
deves, sheep,   O 1065 .. *daves*, O 127.
mergh, horses,   O 1065 .. *margh*, O 124.
tel, holes,   D 3174 .. *tol*, D 3170.
escarn, bones,   O 2743 ⎫
yscarn,   D 3173 ⎭ .. *ascorn*, R 2598.

Some end in *n*:—
kuen, dogs,   R 172 from *ky*, R 2026.
lysten, cloths, O 808.
hynwyn, names O 135 from *hanow*, R 1669.

Words from the English generally take *s* in the plural:—

persons,	O 110,	persons.
onours,	D 1627,	honours.
scryptours,	D 1673,	scriptures.
doctours,	D 1626,	doctors.
syres,	D 1471,	sirs.
skorgys, whyppys,	D 2056,	scourges, whips.
chaynys,	D 2060,	chains.

§. 9. What the Welsh and Breton grammarians call the dual number, viz. a compound of the numeral with the noun, used only in the case of parts of the body which are double, is common in Cornish. Example:—*dyulef,* D 2375, *dule,* D 2163, "the hands," from *luef,* "hand," D 2755; *dywscoth,* D 3068, *duscoth,* D 2583, "the shoulders," from *scouth,* D 658; *dywvregh,* D 3159, "the arms," from *bregh,* D 2753; *dewlagas,* "the eyes," D. 396; *dewlyn,* O 1196, *deuglyn,* D. 247, "the knees," &c. &c.

When such parts of the body are mentioned as belonging to more than one person, a plural is used, as *dornow,* "hands," D 1390; also *lagasow,* R 1492, "the eyes" of two men.

§. 10. *Cases.*

With the exception of the genitive, all the cases are formed, as in English, by prepositions; as, *the vyghtern David,* "to king David," O 1929; *yn Araby,* "in Arabia," O 1930; *a'n pen,* "from the head," D 1743; *a dre,* "from home," O 2172; *the'n tas,* "to the father," O 2619.

The genitive of attribution, such as might be rendered by an adjective, is, I think, usually made by a^2; as, *Arluth a ras,* "Lord of grace," R 767, i. e. gracious Lord; *Tas a nef,* "Father of heaven,"

SUBSTANTIVES.

"heavenly Father;" *myghtern a gallos,* "king of power," R 834, powerful king. This is also the form of an ablative case; as, *a'y thywle,* "from his hands," D 3153. But the ordinary genitive is made by apposition only, always following the chief substantive; as, *myghtern yethewon,* "King of the Jews," D 1998; *mab den,* "Son of man," O 1950; *coys Penryn,* "wood of Penryn," O 2589; *taves den,* "tongue of man," O 767. Sometimes the genitive suffers a mutation for no reason that I am aware of, as, *pen vys (mys),* "the end of a month," D 1646; *pen vyghterneth (myghterneth),* "head of royalty," R 313.

I think I have been in error in printing the genitive with the article *a'n* instead of *an.* I did not at first see the difference between the genitive of attribution and the ordinary genitive, and therefore put *a'n* indiscriminately; I now should write *deu a'n nef,* "God of the heaven," O 480, i. e. "heavenly God," but *cusil an tas,* "counsel of the father," O 188.

§. 11. One of the most interesting peculiarities of the Cornish language, which distinguishes it from the cognate Welsh and Armoric and connects it with the Gaelic dialects, is the possession of a really inflected genitive case formed by internal vocalic change, of precisely the same nature as the Irish genitive. It is true that I find no example of this genitive in the ancient Manuscripts, but it certainly existed in the modern Cornish a century and half ago, when Lhuyd wrote his Archæologia Britannica. The passage shewing this case is found at p. 242, and I quote it here:

"They used formerly, and do yet in several words, a variation of vowel (whether the first or the only one) in the genitive case, &c.

"Particularly *a*, I find changed into *e*; as *Marh*, A horse; *Rên verh*, Horse mane; *Buzl verh*, Horse dung; and *e* into *i, y*, or *ey*: as *Merh*, A daughter; *An vyrh*, Of the daughter; *Pen*, A head; *Er dha byn*, Against thee, *q. d.* On thy head; And *Er agas pyn huy*, Against you; *Huêl*, Work; *Mein hueyl*, Work stones, or stones for Building; *Krês*, The midst; *In kreys an dre*, In the midst of the Town."

Now this is precisely the Gaelic genitive, as found in the oldest Irish relics, and in the language now spoken; *pyn*, genitive of *pen*, is equivalent in form and meaning to *cinn*, genitive of *ceann*; *marh*, genitive *merh*, is like *clann*, genitive *clainn*; *krês*, genitive *kreys*, is equal to *éan*, genitive *éin*.

In the compound preposition *erbyn* (from *er pen*), "against," a trace of this change is found even in Welsh, though the Welsh grammarians do not notice it. Lhuyd was led to the discovery of the nature of this compound preposition by finding its parts separated in the Cornish manuscripts, and a governed pronoun inserted between them, though he says nothing of its analogy to his own language, or to Irish. A Cornish man would say *erbyn haf*, "against summer," O 31, as it is in Welsh; but he would say *er ow fyn*, "against me," R 1919, 2573; *er the byn*, "against thee," O 1350; *er y byn*, "against him," D 232; *er agan pyn*, "against us," D 1663; *er agas pyn*, "against you," D 180; and *er aga fyn*, "against them," P. 96. 4, with the regular initial changes, shewing the nature of the substantive.

The ancient Irish is perfectly analogous, though the modern dialect does not appear to have retained it so closely; *ar chenn*, literally "to the head," means "in front of," or "against;" *ar mo chiunn*, is "be-

SUBSTANTIVES.

fore me ;" *ar a chiunn*, "before him ;" *ar ar chiunn*, "before us," &c. &c. See Zeuss, pp. 577 and 618.

I have dwelled on this genitive at greater length than might seem called for, because it is the only trace of a declension in the Cymric class of languages, and is decidedly opposed to the theory that cases were developed in Gaelic after the separation of the two families; it impugns also the classification which denies to the Cymric the character of an Indo-germanic tongue, on the grounds of the supposed non-development of declension.

A substantive preceding another in the genitive case never takes the article: as *map deu*, "the Son of God," D 1951; *both ow thas (tas)*, "the will of my Father," R 157; *gos ow holon (colon)*, "the blood of my heart," R 166; *gorfen beys*, "the end of the world," D 1704.

§. 12. The dative case is formed by *the*[2], or *the* with the second form; as *the dre (tre)*, " to town," O 906; *the gyk (kyk)*, " to flesh ;" *the woys (goys)*, " to blood," O 66.

The ablative also takes the second form, as *a vaghtyth (maghtyth)*, " from a virgin," D 3027.

The vocative preceded by a personal pronoun or by *a*, takes also the second form : as, *a vap (map)*, " O son," O 1336; *a vam (mam)*, " O mother," D 2949; *ty venen (benen)*, " thou woman," R 917; *ty vaow (maow)*, " thou boy," O 2317.

§. 13. *Derivation of Substantives.*

Abstract substantives are derived from adjectives by adding *ter* after a surd consonant, and *der* after other letters:

20   CORNISH GRAMMAR.

Ex. *dader*, goodness,   D 1296 from *da*, good.
    guyrder, truth,   O 1732 .. *guyr*, true.
    guander, weakness,   D 2618 .. *guan*, weak.
    yender, coldness,   D 1223 .. *yen*, cold.
    golowder, brilliancy,   O 1413 .. *golow*, light.
    tekter, beauty,   D 33   .. *tek*, beautiful.
    whekter, sweetness,   O 359   .. *whek*, sweet.
    uṭhekter, horror,   D 2653 .. *uṭhyk*, frightful,
                                        R 2340, *uṭhek*, O 798.
    melder, sweetness,   R 457   .. *mel*, honey.

Adjectives in *s*, anciently ending with *t*, recover the *t* in becoming substantives; as,

    caletter, hardness, O 1524, from *cales*, hard, O 1525, D 927.
    goscotter, shelter, O 361, is the probable reading from *guskys*, O 356, the Welsh *gwasgod*.
    ponvotter, trouble, O 363, from *ponvos*, R 1327, but these two examples are hardly regular, the roots having rather the value of substantives.

Other abstract substantives take *eth* or *neth*[a], but their simpler form is more commonly a substantive:—

    guyryoneth, truth,   D 2029 from *guyryon*, true men.
    cosoleth, rest,   O 1725 .. *cosel*, O 2073.
    skentuleth, wisdom,   D 1809.
    bolungeth, will,   D 2053.
    myghterneth, royalty,   R 313   .. *myghtern*, a king.
    folneth, folly,   R 961   .. *fol*, R 953, a fool.
    gokyneth, stupidity,   D 1808 .. *goky*, O 173, a fool.
    muscoghneth, madness, D 1990 .. *muscok*, crazed, D 961.
    gowegneth, falsehood,   R 906   .. *gowek*, a liar, R 55.
    roweth, bounty,   O 884   .. *ro*, a gift, O 2467.

Abstract substantives derived from verbs commonly end in *ans*:—

---

[a] Welsh and Armoric analogy would require *eṭh*, but Lhuyd wrote always *eth*. See his Grammar, p. 240.

SUBSTANTIVES. 21

crygyans, belief,	D 1813	from	*crygy.*
gyvyans, forgiveness,	D 1816	..	*gafa.*
dysquythyans, declaration,	O 1733	..	*dysquethya.*
gorthyans, worship,	O 1738	..	*gorthe.*
bewnans, life,	O 848 ⎫	..	*bewe*, to live.
bewnens, ..	O 701 ⎭		
mernans, death,	O 1522	..	*maruel.*
sylwans, salvation,	O 1958	..	*sylwel.*
sylwyans, ..	R 2611.		
trystyns, sadness,	D 1023.		

Arlottes, "a lordship," D 1614, is from *arluṯh*, "a lord;" *wythres*, "a work," or thing made, O 1069, 1853, from *wyth*, "the doing," O 2572, D 3029, is analogous to the Welsh *gwaith* and *gweithred*.

A substantive signifying a doer is sometimes made by adding *or* to a verb or noun, as *tyor*, "a tiler," O 2486, from *ty*, "to cover," O 2475. See also *pystryor*, "a wizard," D 1767, from *pystry*, "sorcery," D 1765.

In the ancient vocabulary several such names of agency end in *iad* or *iat*. Similar forms become in the dramas *guythyas*, "a keeper," O 692; *sylvyas*, "a saviour," D 252, R 307.

We have a termination *va* in *powesva*, "rest," O 145; *cofva*, "remembrance," D 827, and *dywethva*, "end," D 728.

It may be given as a rule without exception, that words ending with *t* or *d* in Welsh or Breton, do, if they exist in Cornish, turn *t* or *d* to *s*; and this whether genuine Celtic, or borrowed from Latin or English; as, *nans*, "a valley;" *goys*, "blood;" *gwyls*, "grass;" *guyns*, "wind;" *ros*, "net;" *pons*, "bridge;" *tas*, "father;" *spyrys*, "spirit," corresponding with *nant*, *gwaed*, *gwellt*, *gwynt*, *rhwyd*, *pont*, *tad*, *yspryd*.

§. 14. ADJECTIVES.

The adjective usually follows the substantive, and if the latter be a feminine singular, the adjective takes the second form, when the initial is mutable. Examples are, "*gobar bras*, "great reward," R 672; *mor ruyth*, "red sea," O 1622; *merkyl tek*, "fair miracle," O 1450; *luef gleth (cleth)*, "left hand," D 2747; *cusyl tha (da)*, "good advice," O 2802; *benen vas (mas)*, "good woman," R 1697. In *guyr vres*, "true judgment," D 515, and *guyr gos*, "true blood," D 1506, the adjective precedes.

According to Lhuyd, p. 243, an adjective with *y* for its vowel was made feminine by changing *y* to *e*; as, *guyn*, m. *guen*, f. "white;" *melyn*, m. *melen*, f. "yellow." I do not know sufficiently the genders of nouns, and adjectives are not of very frequent occurrence, so that I have not noticed the change; but it is consistent with Welsh Grammar.

The comparative and superlative degrees both end in *a* (*e*) without distinction; as, *brasa*, "greater," from *bras*, D 793; *uhella*, "highest," D 2189, from *uhel*, O 805; or *lelle*, "more faithful," O 1111, from *lel*. The finals *ch* and *f* (*m*), which make a difference between the degrees in Welsh and Armoric, have disappeared in Cornish, though in the last days of its existence Lhuyd added an apostrophe or *h* to shew the comparative. The adjective in these stages appears to come rather before than after the substantive. Example:— *Uhella arloth*, "most high Lord." D 2189; *gokye den*, "most foolish man," R 1454; *lacka mester*, "a worse master," D 2275; *lelle ethen*, "more

NUMBERS. 23

faithful bird," O 1111; *tekke alter*, "a fairer altar," O 1177; *brasa gallos*, "greatest power," D 793; *guel guyn*, "better wine," O 1914; but we find also *guyn guella*, "best wine," O 1904; *dyllas guella*, "best clothes," D 256.

"Than" after a comparative is made by *ys*, *es*, or *ages*. Example:—*whekke ys mel*, "sweeter than honey," R 144; *moy es spencer*, "greater than a butler," D 802; *teke ages kyns*, "fairer than before," D 348.

Some comparatives appear to have no root extant; as, *guel* or *guella*, "better;" *gueth*, "worse," R 2026, and perhaps *guetha*, D 1130; *moy*, O 1414; *mogha*, D 510; *moghya*, D 513; *moghye*, D 514, "more or most," and perhaps a few more.

Adjectives are often made from substantives by the addition of *ek* or *yk*. Examples are:—

gallosek,	R 752, powerful,	from	*gallos,* O 1214.
ounek,	D 2158, fearful,	..	*oun,* O 1452.
lowenek,	R 1333, joyful,	..	*lowene,* D 574.
marthusek	R 1176, wonderful,	..	*marthys,* O 756.
morethek,	D 3187, mournful,	..	*moreth,* O 358.
ponfosyk,	R 1256, troubled,	..	*ponfos,* R 1327.
anfusyk,	R 1520, mischievous,	..	*anfus,* D 1501.
whansek,	D 37, desirous,	..	*whans,* O 1806.
dyscrygyk,	R 1369, incredulous,	from the verb *crygy*, to believe.	

§. 15. NUMBERS.

The following list of cardinal numbers is partly from the Manuscripts, and where no authority is cited, from the list published by Pryce; the words between brackets are intended as corrections of the loose forms given in Pryce's list, made by the analogies of Welsh and Armoric.

1. *un*, D. 160, 446, with a substantive.
   onan, O 3. *onon*, R 1403, alone.
2. *deu*, D 2577. *dyw*, O 1690. *dew*, R 315.
3. *try*, m. R 374, 870.
   tyr, f. O 828. *tyyr*, f. O 1729. *ter*, f. D 147.
4. *peswar*, m. R 563.
   pedyr, f. O 772.
5. *pymp*, D 505. *pym*, R 867.
6. *whe*, D 351.
7. *seyth*, O 599. *syth*, R 2494.
8. *eath*, (*eyth*.)
9. *naw*, R 661.
10. *dek*, D 574.
11. *ednack*, (*unnek*.)
12. *dewṭhek*, D 228.
13. *tardhak, treṭhek*.
14. *puzwarthack*, (*peswarṭhek*.)
15. *pymṭhek*, P. 228, 1.
16. *huettag, whettak*, (*wheṭhek*.)
17. *seitag*, (*seytek*.)
18. *eatag*, (*eyṭhek*.)
19. *nawnzack*, (*naunṭhek*.)
20. *iganz*, (*ugens*.)
21. *wonnan war iganz*, (*onan war ugens*.)
30. *dek warnugens*, D 593. *dek warnugans*, D 1554.
40. *deu ugens*, D 45. *deu hugens*, R 2437.
46. *dew ugens ha whe*, D 351.
50. *dég ha duganz*, (*dek ha deugans*)
    or *hanter cans*, O 957.
60. *tri iganz*, (*try ugens*), P 227, 3.
70. (*try ugens ha dek*.)
80. *padgwar iganz*, (*peswar ugens*.)
90. *padgwar iganz ha dék*, (*peswar ugens ha dek*)
100. *cans*, D 506. *can*, R 515.
200. *dew cans*, O 657.
300. *try cans*, D 536. *trey hans*, O 1996.
     try hans, O 955.
500. *pymp cans*, D 505.
700. *syth cans*, R 2494.
900. *naw cans*, C. p. 142.

1000. *myl*, D 212. R 348.
 dek can, D 574.
5000. *pymp myl*, P 227, 2.
7000. *syth myl*, R 2494.
100,000. *cans vyl*, O 1614.
1,000,000. *myl vyl*, R 132.
 mylyon, R 2258.

It will be observed that the awkward composition of numbers between ten and fifteen used in Welsh is avoided in Cornish as it is in Armoric; though it is retained in numbers above twenty. The singular Welsh mode of making the numbers between fifteen and twenty is unknown here. The Cornish has retained the distinction of genders in the numerals three and four, but in "two" it seems to have been lost, though retained in Welsh and Armoric.

We have the plural of *myl* in the Creation, p. 54, *moy es millyow a bynsow*, "more than thousands of pounds."

Substantives following the numerals are put in the singular number; as, *naw alweth*, "nine keys," R 661; *deu ladar*, "two thieves," D 2577; *dew ugens dyth*, "forty days," O 1027.

When numbers are compounded, the substantive is placed after the first; as, *dew ugens blythen ha whe*, "forty and six years," D 351.

Ordinal numbers, after the earlier ones, are formed by adding *ves* to the cardinals; *ves* is clearly the Armoric *ved* and Welsh *fed*; it may have been a corruption of *guyth*, "a time," in Welsh *gwaith*.

1st. *kensa*, D 795.
2nd. *secund*, O 17.
 nessa in Pryce's list.
3rd. *tresse*, O 25. *trege*, R 339. *tryge*, R 452.
4th. *peswere*, O 33. *pyswere*, D 2851.
5th. *pympes*, O 41.

6th. *whefes,* O 49.
7th. *seythves,* O 144.
8th. *eathas, (eythves.)*
9th. *nawas.*
10th. *degves,* O 426.

All the rest have *vas* in the lists; the analogy of the Welsh and Armoric, and the *seythves* of the MS. for *seithvas* of the list, show *ves* to be the true form.

§. 16. PERSONAL PRONOUNS.

Personal pronouns may be practically considered as indeclinable; it is true that some of them have two forms, but the second of these is not so much that of an accusative case, as a changed form required by position in respect to its regimen; in the same way the French *moi* and *toi* are not so much the accusative cases of *je* and *tu,* as the forms used when they are less closely connected with a verb than those called exclusively nominatives; it is true that *je* and *tu* are nominatives, and that *moi* and *toi* are generally accusatives; but these are also sometimes nominatives, and this is the case with Cornish personal pronouns. These two forms I would name the first and second states. When personal pronouns follow certain particles ending with vowels, they are abbreviated and otherwise altered; this I would call a third state: when connected with a preposition, they are also abbreviated, but in a different way, which may be termed a fourth state. It will be more intelligible if all the forms be put together in a table, to which it will be convenient to add the possessive pronoun, because the strictly personal pronouns sometimes put on the possessive form.

	1	2	3	4	possess.
I	my, me	vy	'm	'f, 'm	ow³
Thou	ty	sy, gy	'd, 'th	's	the²
He	ef	ef, e	'n	'o	y²
She	hy	hy, y	's	'y	y³
We	ny	ny	'n	'n	agan
You	why	why	's	'ugh	agas
They	y	y	's	'e	aga³

When a personal pronoun is used alone, or when it is the subject of a verb, it is put in the first state: as,

> *my a vyn*, I will, O 2283.
> *me re goskes*, I have slept, R 511.
> *ha my ynno ef*, and I in him, R 2387.
> *ty yu*, thou art, R 751.
> *a ty Iacob*, O thou James, R 1007.
> *ty re wruk*, thou hast done, O 2243.
> *ty ha'th wrek*, thee and thy wife, D 685.
> *ef a vyn*, he will, O 2427.
> *ef hag ol*, he and all, D 636.
> *hy a torse*, she would break, O 2174.
> *ny a'n tregh*, we will cut it, O 2533.
> *why a'n pren*, you shall pay it, R 621.
> *why losels*, you rogues, D 2589.
> *y a'n guanas*, they pierced him, R 1117.

> *Hy* sometimes stands for the neuter, where in English we should use 'it;' as, *kyns hy bos nos*, "before it be night," O 2769.

When the personal pronouns come after verbs, they take the second state; in most of the following examples they come after imperatives: as,

> *gas vy*, let me, O 2703.
> *guyth vy*, preserve me, R 1564.

the naghe gy, to deny thee, R 1156.
kychough ef, catch him, D 1007.
gorreugh ef, put him, R 2077.
synsew e, hold him, D 1086.
lath e, kill him, D 2356.
hertheugh hy, thrust her, R 2295.
lath ny, kill us, O 972.
na blamyowg ny, do not blame us, R 649.
gor y, put them, O 334.
gura y, make them, D 2674.

In the following examples they follow verbs used as conditionals or subjunctives, or they are used by way of emphasis, or perhaps merely from the necessities of metre: as,

ny welaf vy, I do not see, R 1962.
ma thyllyf vy, that I go, R 182.
may fythe gy, that thou mayest be, O 1327.
prag y whruste sy, why didst thou? O 277.
may tebbro ef, that he may eat, O 200.
bys may cothe hy, until she fall, O 2718.
fatel wrussyn ny, how that we did, R 1341.
dun ny, let us go, O 2325.
ny wreugh why, ye do not, O 317.
may fewg why, that ye may be, O 1163.
may fens y, that they may be, O 1833.
may fons y, that they may be, O 2424.

When the personal pronoun is the object of a verb in the indicative or subjunctive mood, in which case the verb is usually preceded by a particle ending with a vowel, the pronoun is abbreviated as in the third column, and affixed to the particle, making one word with it. In this book the particle is separated from the pronoun by an apostrophe for the guidance of the reader, as is done in Welsh, though no such division is found in the Manuscripts. Examples:—

del y'm kyrry, as thou lovest me, O 2403.
aban y'm sawyas, since he healed me, O 1774.

PRONOUNS.   29

me a'th cusyl, I advise thee, R 1130.
my a'd pys, I pray thee, O 2521.
an laddron a'n dyalas, the thieves mocked him, R 1426.
ha re'n dros, and hast brought him, O 282.
my ny'n guylys, I did not see him, D 1286.
my a's guysk, I will strike her, O 2709.
my a's henow, I name her, O 114.
hag a'n doro, and will bring us, O 225.
re'n sawye, may it save us, O 1088.
mar a's guel, if he see you, D 1003.
my a's gueres, I will cure you, O 2017.
me a's ygor, I will open them, R 638.
mar ny's cafaf, if I find them not, R 647.
homma re's holhas, she has washed them, D 520.

There is an indeterminateness about the pronouns in this state, *n* signifying "him" as well as "us," and *s* belonging to three different persons; this has probably led writers in most cases to take the possessive forms, either directly or with some modification, in the first and second persons plural; as, *ef a gan formyas*, "he created us," R 2430; *a gan gruk*, "who made us all," R 1975; *y gen lowenhas*, "he gladdened us," R 1444; *my a gas pys*, "I pray you," O 2346; *re ges bo*, "be it on you," O 2585; *ma gys byth*, "that there be to you," O 348.

When a personal pronoun comes before a verb as its complement, without such particle as is mentioned in the preceding paragraph, it takes the form of the possessive. Examples:—

re ruk ow tholle (tolle), hath deceived me, O 286.
the rewardye my a ra, I will reward thee, O 2310.
me ny fynnaf y grygy (crygy), I will not believe it, R 1047.
greugh y tenne, do ye drag him, R 2232.
worth hy thempte (tempte), to tempt her, O 303.
hy frenne (prenne), to take it, R 2234.
worth agan dry alemma, for carrying us hence, R 151.

30   CORNISH GRAMMAR.

ef a ruk agan dyfen, he did forbid us, O 182.
agan cuthe guren, let us cover ourselves, O 254.
pan wruge ages danvon, when I did send you, D 913.
war beyn agas bos leṭhys, on pain that you be killed, O 2556.
my a vyn aga threhy (trehy), I will cut them, O 1735.
aga guelas o trueth, to see them was pitiful, R 899.

These pronouns may in fact be considered as possessives, coming as they do before infinitives, which are really verbal nouns.

§. 17. *Pronouns with Prepositions.*

Many prepositions coalesce with the pronouns which they govern, forming with them one word. In this case some euphonic artifice is used to unite the two elements into a well-sounding compound: a consonant is doubled or omitted, or a syllable is added, and the vowels undergo the changes described in §. 3. I give here examples of the various modes; and it will be seen that the pronouns are represented in these compounds by the following letters: *m* or *f*, "me;" *s*, "thee;" *o*, "him;" *y*, "her;" *n*, "us;" *ugh*, "you;" *e*, "them," as given in the fourth column of the table in the preceding section.

The prepositions exemplified are *yn*, "in;" *rag*, "for, before;" *dre*, "by, through;" *gans*, "by, with;" *war*, "upon;" *a*, "from;" *ṭhe*, "to;" *orth* or *worth*, "towards."

yn, in.		rag, for, before.	
ynnof, in me,	R 707.	*ragof*, for me,	O 139.
ynnos, in thee,	R 757.	*ragos*, for thee,	O 260.
ynno, in him,	D 2157.	*ragtho*, for him,	R 1251.
ynny, in her,	D 2164.	*ragṭhy*, for her.	
ynnon, in us,	R 1321.	*ragon*, for us,	D 174.

PRONOUNS.   31

ynnough, in you.
ynne, in them,   O 2457.

ragough, for you, D 27.
ragthe, for them, O 2456.

ragas in O 1723, 1724, D 265, &c. has certainly nothing to do with *rag*, but is contracted from *re agas*.

dre, by, through.

drethof, by me,   O 134.
drethos, by thee, R 2220.
dretho, by him,   R 1756.
drythy, by her,   O 1668.
drethon, by us.
drethough, by you.
drethe, by them, O 1958.

gans, by, with.

genef, by or with me, O 2192.
genes, .. with thee, O 2169.
ganso, .. with him, R 744.
gynsy, .. with her, O 2764.
genen, .. with us, O 2378.
geneugh,.. with you, R 1797.
ganse, .. with them, O 1613.

gynef, D 564. *gynen*, R 1347.
genaf, O 672. *genogh*, D 184.
gynes, D 191. *gansse*, D 1373.

war, upon.

warnaf, upon me,   O 1344.
warnas, upon thee, O 1015.
warnotho, upon him, O 1539.
warnethy, upon her, O 775.
warnan, upon us,   O 1700.
warnough, upon you, R 1535.
warnethe, upon them, D 2686.

warnogh, D 2626.

a, from, of.

ahanaf, from me,   D 306.
ahanas, from thee, R 1408.
anotho, from him,   R 742.
anethy, from her,   D 923.
ahanan, from us,   O 1101.
ahanough, from you, R 1500.
annethe, from them, O 1952.

ahanes, O 406.
annotho, O 200.
annethy, O 218.

the, to.

thym,   O 2286.
thys,   R 1473.
thotho, O 2500.
thethy, O 2755.
thyn,   R 1483.
theugh, D 2500.
thethe, O 1824.

dym,   D 741, to me.
dys,   O 1969, to thee.
dotho, R 1445, to him.
dethy, D 2202, to her.
dyn,   R 2361, to us.
deugh,   to you.
dethe, R 2600, to them.

thyugh, O 2399; *theygh*, D 4; *thy*, D 2246, *dy*, D 124.

worth, orth, at, to, against.

worthyf, O 170.	*orthyf,* O 2524, to me.
worthys, R 1570.	*orthys,* to thee.
worto, O 222.	*orto,* R 1343, to him.
worty, O 293, D 3069.	*orty,* O 2173, to her.
worthyn, R 1211.	*orthyn,* O 212, to us.
worthough, R 1171.	*ortheugh,* R 195, to you.
worte, O 2476.	*orte,* to them.

Some of these forms receive an additional syllable, either by way of emphasis, or for filling up a line; we have *thymmo,* O 2256, or *thymo,* O 2333, "to me;" *thyso,* O 2433, or *dyso,* O 2191, "to thee;" *thynny,* "to us," R 626. Sometimes the pronoun is repeated in the second state, as *thymmo vy,* R 446; *thyso gy,* O 2246; *dyso sy,* O 842; *ynno ef,* R 2387; *worty hy,* O 269; *thynny ny,* R 568; *theugwhy why,* O 2209; *annethe y,* O 1952.

§. 18. *Possessive Pronouns.*

These pronouns are placed in the last column of the table in p. 27, but are repeated here for convenience:—*ow*³, "my;" *the*², "thy;" *y*², "his;" *y*³, "her;" *agan,* "our;" *agas,* "your;" *aga*³, "their;" and the pronoun of the second state may or may not follow the noun.

ou thermyn (termyn), my time, O 2344.
ow feryl (peryl) vy, my peril, O 197.
the vap (map), thy son, O 2341.
y gorf (corf), his body, O 2367.
y voth (both) ef, his will, O 483.
y feghas (peghas), her sins, D 528.
hy huth (cuth) hy, her affliction, O 297.
agan lef, our voice, O 2027.
agan arluth ny, our Lord, R 1655.
agen ehen, our class, O 2066.

PRONOUNS.

agas myghtern, your king, O 2348.
agys crygyans, your belief, R 2389.
ages ancow, your death, R 612.
ages guyth why, your keeping, R 651.
aga threys (treys), their feet, O 760.

The possessive, like the personal pronouns, combine with certain prepositions: chiefly *a*, " of " or " from ;" *yn*, " in," and *the*, " to ;" also with the conjunction *ha*, " and ;" *ow* is then changed to *m*, making *thu'm*, " to my," (distinct from *thym*, " to me,") *y'm*, " in my ;" *a'm*, " of my ;" *ha'm*, " and my." *The*, " thy," throws away the vowel in the same cases; the other possessives, beginning with vowels, suffer no change, except that *agas* and *agan* may lose the initial vowel. I do not know whether *agan*, " of our," *agas*, " of your," should be so written, or *a gan, a gas*; they should be joined perhaps in the ordinary genitive, which requires no preposition, and divided where *a* means rather " out of " or " from." See p. 16.

Thum gulas, to my country, R 879.
y'm colon, in my heart, R 760.
a'm offryn, of my offering, O 530.
a'm cleves, of my malady, O 2631.
ha'm gorty, and my husband, O 181.
the'th corf, to thy body, R 487.
a'd pehosow, of thy sins, O 2259.
y'th tour, in thy palace, O 2389.
ha'th vaw (maw), and thy boy, D 2236.
a'y passon, of his passion, R 759.
th'y wleth (guleth), to his kingdom, O 2370.
th'y thyskyblon (dyskyblon), to his disciples, R 794.
ha'y volnogeth (bolnogeth), and his will, O 2352.
ha'y avalow, and its fruits, O 176.
th'agan dysyr, to our desire, R 1206.
d'agan arluth, to our lord, O 2580.
y gen lyfryow, in our books, R 2411.
a gys company, of your company, D 868.
y ges golok, into your sight, R 1861.

war gas flehes, on your children, D 2643.
h'agas myghtern, and your king, O 2348.
h'aga hynwyn, and their names, O 35.

A possessive followed by *honan* (*honon*) becomes the more intense personality which we render by "myself, himself," &c. I do not think it is ever the reflected pronoun.

my a vyn mos ow hon..n, I will go myself, D 87.
ow colon ow honan, my heart of myself, or my own heart, R 2042.
the honan, thyself, O 1455.
the honyn, thyself, O 345.
y honan, himself, R 2065, 2073.
agan honan, ourselves, O 16.
agas honon, yourselves, D 545.
ages honan, yourselves, R 642.

§. 19. *Demonstratives.*

The adjectival demonstrative pronouns are *ma* (*me*) and *na* (*ne*), suffixed to the substantive they refer to. I have, in the text, divided them from their substantives with a hyphen, but in the Manuscript they are written in one word. There is no distinction between singular and plural. Example:

yn bys-ma, in this world, O 1886.
an guel-ma, these rods, O 1739.
yn ur-na, in that hour, D 1899.
yn wlas-na, in that country, R 2461.
yn uur-ne, in that hour, D 1372.

Sometimes *keth* is added, to make the demonstrative more definite, as,

an keth den-ma, this very man, D 1590.
an keth deu-na, that same God, O 1485.
an keth re-na, those very (persons), O 1879.

Sometimes the *m* is doubled, as in *dremme*, "this town," O 2284; *dremma*, "these places," O 2771;

chymma, D 667, *chemma*, R 1397, "this house;" and *a lemma*, "from this place," O 446. *Alemma*, "from this place," and *alena*, "from that place," are in frequent use as adverbs, meaning "hence" and "thence."

The substantive demonstratives distinguish the masculine from the feminine:—

hem or *hemma*, m. *hom* or *homma*, f., this.
hen or *henna*, m. *hon* or *honna*, f., that.

Examples—

hem yu marth, this is a miracle, R 654.
me a dyp bos hemma, I swear this is, R 2508.
homma keffrys, this (woman) also, D 519.
hen yu guyr, that is true, R 977.
y volnogeth yu henna, his will is that, O 2352.
hon yu cusyl fyn, that is fine advice, O 2041.
guyr vres yu honna, a true judgment is that, D 515.
honna yw ol the vlamye, she is all to blame, O 266.

§. 20. *Interrogative Pronouns.*

The Interrogative Pronouns are all resolvable to *py* and *pa*, "who," "what."

pan vernans, what (is) the death? R 2047. = *pa* + *an*.
pa han pleyt, what (is) the plight? R 2058.
pandra wylly, what dost thou see? O 801. = *pa* + *an* + *dra*.
pendra wreth, what wilt thou do? R 203.
py nyl a mogha sengys, which one was most bound? D 510.
py gymmys hys, what amount of length? O 2104.

When the pronoun 'who' comes without addition, it appears to be rendered by *pyu*, or *pyw*, either in the nominative or the accusative, as,

pyu a ylta gy bones, who canst thou be? R 2511.
pyw a whyleugh, whom seek ye? D 1109.

but generally *pyu* is equivalent to *py yu,* "who is," as,

pyu myghtern a lowene, who is the King of joy? R 106.
pyu henna, who is that? R 2487.

The addition of *pynag* makes the pronoun indefinite :—

py penag vo, whatever it be, O 1154.
pe penag vo, whatever it be, O 662.
py le penag, whatever place, D 1551.
pyu penagh a len grysso, whoever faithfully believes, R 2466.

This receives sometimes the addition of *ol,* "all."

py penag ol a sconyo, whoever may object, O 2388.
py penag ol a wharfo, whatever may happen, R 671.

When the *p* is doubled, as in *puppenagol, peppenagol,* I think the first syllable is *pup* or *peb,* "all."

Now and then *pynag* comes alone, as,

pynag a wharfo an cas, whatever may be the case, O 1698.
pynag a fo, whatever it be, R 2000.
pynak vo lettrys py lek, whoever he be, lettered or lay, D 681.
penag a wryllyf amme, whomsoever I shall kiss, D 1084.

§. 21. *Relative Pronouns.*

The Relative Pronoun is represented by *a* and *nep* (*neb*) ; as,

a fue genys, who was born, D 1652.
a wruk Moyses the planse, which Moyses did plant, O 1946.
tas a wruk nef, the Father who made heaven, O 1785.
Urry nep o marrek len, Uriah, who was a trusty knight, O 2338.
neb a glewsys, whom thou didst hear, O 224.
the nep yu ioy ow colon, thou who art the joy of my heart, R 456.

Nep often includes the antecedent, like the Latin *qui* :—

neb yu moghya, he who is greatest, D 792.
ha nep na'n gruk, and he who has not done it, R 158.

When the relative is in the accusative case, or is governed by a preposition, a personal pronoun in the required case is sometimes put after the verb, as in the Semitic languages: "whom I saw" is made "who I saw him;" "to whom I spoke," "who I spoke to him:" as,

a thanfonas e, whom he sent, D 1692.
py gansse, by whom, D 1373 (i. e. who by them).

The relative is often omitted, as in English :

ou thus us gene, my people who are with me, D 1122.
the vap Ysac yw the ioy, thy son Isaac, who is thy joy, O 1374.
yn le na fue den bythqueth, in a place where man never was, D 3135.

Nep is also an indefinite pronoun :—
yn nep fos, in any wall, O 2458.

See also *nep peyth a oel a vercy*, "some of the oil of mercy," O 327; *nebes*, in D 208, 495, is probably a mere contraction of *nep peyth*.

Myns may be considered as a relative pronoun, including in itself the antecedent 'all,' like our word 'whatever.'

keusyns den myns a vynno, let a man say all that he will, R 2448.
hag ol myns o, and every thing that was, R 127.
myns yu guyryon, whoever are innocent, R 163.
rak kuthe myns us formyys, to cover all that is created, O 22.
ty a fyth mens a vynny, thou shalt have whatever thou wilt, D 590.

Kemmys, kymmys, "as many as," or "whosoever," the Armoric *kement* and Welsh *cymmaint*, is frequently used:

kemmys re wruk both ow thas, as many as have done the will of my father, R 157.
kemmys na greysa, whoever believes not, R 176.

It is used as a substantive in *py gymmys hys,* "what amount of length," O 2104.

Kynyver is like *kemmys:*—*kynyver peyn us yn beys,* "any punishment there is in the world," R 2055; *kynyver best us yn tyr,* "as many beasts as are in the world," O 1215; see O 1029.

Suel is another relative rarely used; the Welsh *sawl.* I find only one case of its employment: *py suel a vynnyth,* "whatever thou wilt," D 592.

It is possible that *sul a the'n nef* in R 136., (*sul* for *suel*,) which I have made "going up to heaven," may be "who is going to heaven." In Mount Calvary *suel* is used at least three times: in 2. 1.[a] and 79. 2, where we have *suell a vynno,* it means "he who;" in 119. 4, *suel a wresse,* "that which."

§. 22. *Miscellaneous Pronouns.*

The following have been observed in going over the text, but it is not believed that these are all.

"The one" and "the other," when opposed, are sometimes made by *nyl* and *gyle:*—*an nyl a delle pymp cans, ha hanter cans y gyle,* "the one owed five hundred, and a half hundred the other," D 504, 506; *me a gylm an nyl, ha me a gylm y gyle,* "I will bind the one, and I will bind the other," D 2785, 2788.

---

[a] Misprinted *cuell,* which misled Zeuss.

PRONOUNS.

Sometimes "the other" is made by *aral*, in plural *erel*:—*an nyl torn y fyth re hyr, tres aral re got*, "at one hand it is too long, by the other too short," O 2548, 2549.

Aral is always used with a substantive:

ioseph ha tus erel, Joseph and other persons, R 3.
en thyu grous erel, the two other crosses, D 2820.
ple kefyr dyu grous aral, where may two other crosses be found, D 2576.

In this last example *aral* may be put in the singular for the sake of the rhyme; this would be admissible in consequence of the singular form of the preceding word after a numeral; as also in *lyes profus aral*, "many other prophets," R 1485.

In Armoric, *ébén* is used for "the other," when feminine; and I believe the following lines contain cases of a similar pronoun in Cornish:—

My a dyl tol rak hybeen, "I will bore a hole for the other," D 2749, follows a line by another speaker, *me a teyl tol rag an nyl*, "I will bore a hole for the one," D 2743. As the allusion is to the feminine noun *luef*, "the hand," there cannot be much doubt in the case.

In *why drehevough ybeyn*, "you raise the other," D 2826, the case is not so sure, because the allusion may be either to the man or the cross; both are mentioned, but *crous* is a feminine noun.

In the third case, *ty a theg a neyl pen, cachaf yben*, "thou carry one end, I will seize the other," O 2816, *pen* is masculine; so that either the Cornish does not follow the Armoric, or the last clause will awkwardly mean "I will seize its end."

The word *ken*, which is usually a conjunction, as in D 481, is also used for 'other;' as,

nag us ken deu agesos, there is no other God than thou, R 2477.

CORNISH GRAMMAR.

a wylsta ken, dost thou see any other thing, O 795.
the ken pow, to another country, R 2218.
yn ken lyw, in another colour, R 2534.

"Any" is made by *nep*, which is placed before the substantive it refers to ; as,

yn nep maner, in any way, R 497.
yn neb gulas, in any land, O 1120.
yn nep fos, in any wall, O 2458.

"Any" may also be made by *byth*, placed after the substantive ; as,

den vyth, O 2457, or *den fyth*, any man, D 1481.
trumeth vyth, any mercy, O 1650.
mar quren flogh vyth denythy, if we do any children produce, O 390.

Ol added to *byth* makes it more indefinite, as,

den byth ol, any man whatever, R 2169.
onan vyth ol, any one of them, O 1697.
mar pyth drok vyth ol gureys, if any evil is done, O 601.

Pup, "all," is used alone, or with a substantive; and sometimes with the addition of *ol* :—

yn pup tra, in all things, O 2354.
guetyeugh pup y worthye, take care all to worship it, O 2555.
pup den ol, all men, O 1043, D 1905.
war pep ol marnas ty, over all but thee, O 948.
gans pup ol, by every body, R 1096.
pup huny, every one, O 969, 2017.

Ol is used in the same way :

gulan yu ol, all are clean, D 864.
ol the chy, all thy house, O 2340.
arluth dres ol an bys-ma, lord above all this world, D 1683.

Kettep, "every :"

marow vethyn kettep pen, dead we shall be every head, O 1655.
yn kettep pen, every head, D 762.
kettep onan, every one, D 2821.

Lyes, lues, "many," is used with a substantive singular:—

yn lyes le, in many places, D 749.
ynno lues trygva, in it many dwellings, O 951.
lyes profus aral, many other prophets, R 1485.

Re is like a substantive, meaning "persons" or "things:"

an re-ma yu oberys, these (things) are made, O 15.
cafus re me a vyn, take those (persons) I will, R 184.
an keth re-na, these same (men), O 1897.
the wruthyl gans an re-na, to do with them, D 182.

---

§. 23. VERBS.

The Cornish verb, in conjugation, in forms, and in the number and use of its tenses, approaches more nearly to the Armoric than to the Welsh verb, though some of its forms are more like those of the latter dialect.

Every verb may be conjugated in three different modes; in the first, which I call the Inflected conjugation, every tense and person has its own form, as in Latin and Greek, and it is equally rare to find a personal pronoun used as it is in those languages; it is not done unless emphasis be required; as, *my ny gresaf,* "*I* will not believe (if *you* do), R 904.

The present tense of the verb *care,* "to love," is in this mode of conjugating made, *caraf, keryth, car, keryn, carough, carans.*

In the second mode, which Breton grammarians call the Impersonal conjugation, the third person singular is taken for the whole tense, and the persons are distinguished by the added pronoun, as in English and French. The present tense is thus, *my a gar, ty a gar, ef a gar, ny a gar, why a gar, y a gar; car* becomes *gar* by the influence of the affirmative a^2, used when the subject precedes the verb.

In the third mode, which may be conveniently called the Compound conjugation, the auxiliary "to do" accompanies the verb to be conjugated, precisely in the same manner as is done in the English, "I do love," &c. The sole difference is, that the Cornish extends this addition of the auxiliary verb to cases where we do not use it; saying not only "I do love" and "I did love," but also "I will do love." The first tense would thus be generally, *my a wra care*, "I do love," *ty a wra care*, "thou dost love;" and if used personally, which is less frequently done, *guraf care, gureth care*, &c.

There can be no doubt that these various modes show a corruption in the language, which the more classical Welsh would disdain; but it appears practically to have conferred facilities in the expression of certain modifications of meaning, akin to those we find in English from the use of 'might,' 'could,' 'would,' 'should,' &c., which the stiffer forms of Latin, or even German, would hardly admit of.

§. 24. We may here notice what are called by Zeuss the verbal particles, y^2, a^2, and re^2. *Y* and *a* are used only in affirmative sentences, and the chief difference I find between them is that *a* is used where the nominative case precedes the verb, as in *me a wra (gura)*, "I will do," R 1755; *ef a vynse (mynse)*, "he would have wished," O 2224; *urry a fyth (byth) lethys*, "Uriah shall be killed," O 2123; and *y* where the nominative either follows or is omitted; as, *y fyen lethys*, "I should be killed," O 2120; *y ma moyses pel gyllys*, "Moses is gone far," O 1682.

I did not discover until a good deal of the work was printed, that *yth*, which frequently occurs, is a mere euphonic change of *y* before a vowel: see *yth arghaf*, "I command," O 381; *yth ymwanas*, "he stabbed himself," R 2065; *yth emwyskys*, "he smote himself," R 2067; *yth af*, "I will go," R 2400, &c. &c. In *ythanwaf* (=*yth hanwaf*,) O 123, and *ytheuel*, O 19, an *h* is omitted; see *yth heuel*, R 2491. In like manner the participal *ow*^{3} (see below, in the participles,) may become *owth* before a vowel, as in *outh emloth*, D 2509, *owth ysethe*, D 2342, *outh ymwethe*, ("craving," from the Welsh *ymhwedd*) R 1170, *owth egery*, "opening," D 2999; and the conjecture hazarded in the note on D 932 will be well founded. As in the case of *y*, there is the omission of *h* in *outhenwel* (=*outh henwel*), O 2729.

The use of the particle *re* will be given under the Third tense

§. 25. *Tenses.*

There are five tenses, analogous in form, though slightly differing in value, to those of Welsh and Armoric verbs. I distinguish them by numbers, to avoid any ambiguity which might attend the varying practice of writers on Celtic grammar. No distinct division of moods is made here, because many of the forms are used as indicatives as well as subjunctives.

The First tense is used for present or future time. The termination of the first person was *af* in the three languages, though the Bretons now write *ann*. The Welsh use this tense almost always as a future, expressing the present by a periphrasis: the Bretons keep to the present time, and use the Fifth tense as a future; in Cornish it is most commonly used for present time: the frequent use of the Compound conjugation enabled the Cornishman to make a separate future, though he still continued to use the First tense for future time occasionally. Taking the verb *care*, "to love," as our example, the present tense is—

caraf, keryth, car : keryn, carough, carons.

The Second tense is the imperfect of Welsh and Breton grammarians; Zeuss named it the secondary present. It is sometimes used as an indicative, sometimes as an optative or subjunctive, a potential or a conditional. This vagueness is unnecessary in Cornish, because the Compound conjugation gives a fair conditional; but the Cornish writers nevertheless retained the variety of meaning occasionally with the simple form, and even confounded it with the Fourth tense. The first person ends with *en* in Cornish, *enn* in Armoric, and *wn* in Welsh. The whole tense is made—

caren, cares, care (cara) : caren, careugh, carens.

The Third tense is the Preterite, and its use is the same in the three languages. The first person ends in *ys* in Cornish, *ais* in Welsh, and *iz* in Armoric. The whole tense is—

kerys, kersys, caras : kersyn, carsough, carsons(ans).

The Fourth tense is named the Preterpluperfect in Welsh and Armoric; Zeuss called it the secondary perfect. Its use in those languages is in ac-

TENSES. 45

cordance with its name, but it is more commonly employed as a subjunctive or conditional. In Cornish, so far as I have observed, it is used as a conditional only, and it is frequently confounded with the second tense. The first person in Cornish ends with *sen*, in Welsh with *swn*, in Armoric *zenn*. The whole tense is—

carsen, carses, carse : carsen, carseugh, carsens.

The Fifth tense is a subjunctive present or future in Cornish, and in Welsh, I believe, rather future than present; in Armoric it is the Future indicative. The respective terminations of the first person are *yf, wyf, if* (*inn*). The plural of this tense is often confounded with that of the Second tense, and it will be seen generally that there is a good deal of irregularity in the inflections, which makes the paradigm given rather theoretically than practically exact. The whole tense is—

kyryf, kyry, caro : kyryn, kyreugh, carons.

The Imperative is—

car, cares or *carens : caren, careugh, carens.*

The infinitive takes many forms; sometimes it is the simple root, sometimes a vowel is added to the root, and sometimes *el, es*, &c. In the example given here, the termination is *e*, as *care*.

The active participle is made by prefixing *ow°*, changing a sonant initial to its surd form; as in Armoric, where *o taléa*, "delaying," is from *daléa*, "to delay."

The passive participle ends in *ys*, as *kyrys*.

The passive verb ends in *er* or *yr*, which by Welsh analogy should designate the present and future tenses; but I find no difference in their use; *er* is far more frequent than *yr*; the past tense ends in *as*, and a conditional is found in *ser*.

§. 26. As the above enumeration differs in some degree from the plan of Lhuyd, I shall give several examples of each form used, when there is any doubt.

I. Tense. First person:—*gowegneth ny garaf* (*caraf*), "I do not love falsehood," R 906; *lavaraf theugh newothow*, "I will tell you news," R 894. In this person *f* is sometimes omitted for the sake of rhyme; as, *ny vynna*, "I will not," O 1330; *a wela*, "I see," O 1396: *lavara*, "I say," O 1645, D 1.

Second person: — *ny geusyth* (*keusyth*, from *cous*), "thou dost not speak," D 2181; *ny a'n tregh del levereth*, "we will cut it as thou sayest," O 2533; *ny'm guelyth arte*, "thou shalt not see me again," O 244.

> Lhuyd makes *i* the termination; but this is the subjunctive.

Third person:—*neb may fe moghya geffys, a gar* (*car*) *moghye*, "he who is forgiven most, loves most," D 513; *mar kyf carynnyas y tryg*, "if he finds carrion he will stay," O 1103, 4.

> It is seen by these examples that some verbs make no change in this form, as *car;* while others, as *kyf* from *caf*, are subject to the rule of §. 3, notwithstanding the absence of a final *i*, which is quite lost in the Cymric dialects, though it existed in the old Irish, as *cairi*, "he loves."

First person plural:—*ny gemeryn* (*kemeryn*) *nep lowene*, "we take not any pleasure," R 2365; *amen pigyn*, "Amen, we pray," D 199; *leveryn ol thotho*, "we will all say to him," D 2880.

> Lhuyd makes this termination *on*.

Second person plural:—*ny wothough* (*gothough*)

TENSES.   47

ow gorthyby, "ye knew not how to answer me," D 1484; *prag yth hembrenkygh*, "why do ye lead? D 204.

<small>Lhuyd ends this in *oh*.</small>

Third person plural:—*ny wothons (gothons) py nyl a wrons*, "they know not what they do," D 2774; *ny'n cresons ef neffre*, "they will never believe it," O 1440.

<small>Lhuyd writes *anz*.</small>

II. Tense. First person; Indicative:—*ny wothyen (gothyen) man*, "I did not know at all," R 2559; *byth ny wylyn (guylyn)*, I did not see any thing," R 434.

Subjunctive: *a's dysken*, "if I take it off," R 1941; *a quellen (guellen) wyth*, "if I could see once," O 685; *py le penag y's kyffyn*, "wherever I find a place," D 1551.

Conditional: *ru'm fay a'n caffen*, "by my faith I would take him," R 289.

Second person; Indicative:—*ny wothas (gothas)*, "thou didst not know," D 2181; *whylyes*, "thou wast seeking," R 1680.

Subjunctive, &c.: *a tryckes yn tre*, "if thou hadst stayed at home," R 1381; (confusion of tense) *ny wothes (gothes) wheth*, "thou mayest not know yet," D 848; *beys vynytha y wharthes (guarthes)*, "for ever thou wouldst laugh," O 153. See also D 2862, 2864, for conditionals ending in *ys*.

Third person:—*hacre mernans ny gaffe den*, "a more cruel death a man may not find," R 2074; *byth wel cusyl a lavarre*, "any better advice who can tell," R 422; *ru'm gorre th'y wlas*, "may he bring me to his country," O 532; *py plas y thylle*, "where he may go," D 635; *kyn y'n carra*, "though he may love him," R 1897; *pan dremenna an bys-ma,* "when this life may pass, O 875; *me a'n gafse a menne gelwel,* "I would forgive him if he would ask," D 1816; *war Ihesu me a cryas thymmo gafe,* "I cried to Jesus that he would forgive me," R 1100; *golow na wella (guella),* "that he may not see light," R 2003.

First person plural:—*na wrellen buthy,* "that we be not drowned," O 1048; *bys venytha na sorren,* "nor should we be troubled for ever," O 220.

> Such forms as *wreny,* D 190, and *veny,* D 604, are probably orthographical variations of *wren ny* and *ven ny.*

Second person plural:—*mas y'm gorthebeugh,* "unless ye answer me," R 47; *pysough na entreugh yn temptacyon,* "pray that ye enter not into temptation," D 1059.

Third person plural:—*avorow thy's may teffens,* "that they come to thee to-morrow," O 2417; *me a vynse a talfens,* "I would they were worth," D 211.

> I believe this is the tense which Lhuyd makes *mai huellam, huellaz, huello, huellan, huelloh, huellanz,* with the exception of *huello.*

III. Tense. First person:—*ol an tekter a wylys (guylys),* "all the beauty that I saw," O 766; *worto y keusys,* "I spoke to him," R 897; *y vyrys y wolyow,* "I saw his wounds," R 898.

Second person:—*tersys an bara,* "thou didst break the bread," R 1318; *mab deu o neb a wylsys (gylsys),* "the Son of God it was whom thou sawest," O 809.

> Lhuyd makes this termination *yst,* which is Welsh rather than Cornish; the Armoric agrees with the Cornish in the insertion of a sibilant.

Third person:—*clewas agan lef,* "he heard our voice," O 2027; *un marrek a'n lathas,* "a horseman slew him," O 2226.

> I am inclined to think that *dorrasa,* in *pan dorrasa an aval,* "when he plucked the apple," O 879, is a subjunctive form of this tense, as in the irregulars *wruge* and *thuhe.*

First person plural:—*leveryn del wylsyn (guylsyn) ny,* "let us speak as we saw," R 807; *an corf a worsyn (gorsyn) yn beth,* "the body which we placed in the tomb," R 49.

Second person plural:—*an onor a wrussough (grussough) thy'mmo,* "the honour which you did to me," D 312; *corf a worseugh (gorseugh) why,* "the body which you placed," R 43.

Third person plural:—*pan y'n lathsons,* "when they killed him," D 3098; *ny torsans chy,* "they did not break the house," R 662.

The addition of the word re^2, corresponding with the old Welsh *ry, re,* now seldom, if ever, used, (see Williams's Dosparth, &c. Llandovery, 1856, pp. 130, 131, and Zeuss, p. 420,) turns this tense into the preterperfect, and was of frequent use in Cornish:—

ef re gollas an plas, he hath lost the place, O 420.
an sarf re ruk ou tholle, the serpent hath deceived me, O 286.
my re wruk prenne, I have redeemed, R 2622.
hy re gafes, she has found, O 1143.

Re is also frequently found with the third person singular of the Second or Fifth tense, in the imperative or optative sense; as, *re'n kergho an dewolow,* "let the devils fetch him," R 2277; *re wronntyo,* "let him grant," O 1726; *re bo,* "let him be," R 2417; *re by gorthys,* "be he worshipped," R

2523; *ru'm gorre*, "may he bring me," O 532. It often occurs in the phrase *ragas bo*, for *re agas bo*, and once, O 1724, in *ragas guytho*. In O 2585 it is written *re ges bo*. The verb *eth*, "he went," takes *s* after *re*: see *re seth*, D 1027, 1246[a].

IV. Tense. First person:—*guelas ow map y carsen*, "I would love to see my son," R 442; *desefsen merwel*, "I would have desired to die," R 1771; *mensen*, "I would wish," R 444.

> In R 289, 290, we have an example of the confusion between this and the Third tense: *a'n caffen, y'n toulsen*, "I would take him, I would cast him." It is possible, however, that the reading may be *cafsen*.

Second person:—*the'n nef grusses yskynne*, "to heaven thou wouldst ascend," O 156.

Third person:—*ny garse pelle bewe*, "he would not like to live longer," O 738; *yn tridyth y'n dreafse*, "in three days he would rebuild it," D 366.

First person plural:—*ny ny'n drosen thy'so gy*, "we would not have brought him to thee," D 1976.

Second person plural:—*pan cleuseugh cous*, "when ye heard speak," D 1338, (may be the Third tense).

Third person plural:—*ny wrussens (grussens) ow dystrewy*, "they would not have destroyed me," D 2777.

> Lhuyd gives a tense corresponding with this in form:— *guelzen, guelzez, guelze : guelzen, guelze', guelzenz*, or

---

[a] This verb, in all its forms beginning with a vowel, takes *s*, or its equivalent *th*, after the conjunction *mar* and some others. In this it is like the vocalic forms of the verb substantive, as well as in its frequent accompaniment of *yth*.

TENSES. 51

guelazzenz: he makes it the preter-pluperfect tense. He also gives a subjunctive future, *guylfym, guylfydh, guylyf; guylfon, guelfo, guylfynz:* this is certainly one of the compounds of the verb substantive, of which there are many in the other dialects as well as in Cornish: *adnabod* in Welsh and *anavout* in Armoric are instances. I think I find *clewfyf,* "I should feel," in O 1351; *clewfo,* "that he may hear," is certainly the reading of D 3063. The Breton makes the conditional in *fenn, zenn,* and *jenn,* indiscriminately. A Cornish future in *fyth (wyth, vyth)* is often found impersonal :—*ty a wylfyth (guylfyth),* "thou shalt see," O 1449; *gothfyth,* "I shall know," O 1400; *me a'n carvyth,* "I will love him," D 1703; *ef a'th carvyth,* "he will love thee," D 1846; *ny a'n guylfyth,* "we shall see it," R 53, &c. &c.

V. Tense. First person :—*worto pan wofynnyf (gofynnyf,)* "of him when I ask," D 1855; *bys may thyllyf,* "until I enter," D 726; *guel ha gyllyf,* "the best that I can," D 3012.

Second person :—*me a'th conjor may leverry,* "I adjure thee that thou tell," D 1323; *gueyt may tanfenny, (danfenny),* "take care that thou send," R 1630.

Third person :—*pyu penagh a len grysso (crysso),* "whosoever shall faithfully believe," R 2466; *a gutho (cutho) ol an nor beys,* "which shall cover all the face of the earth," O 982; *kettyl y'n geffo (keffo) a'n bay,* "when he shall find him, he will kiss him," D 986.

I think I find this form used in the indicative :—*my a's dyllo,* "I will send her," O 1101. We have also *doro* as a future in D 1471; but as we find *doro* in the imperative mood in O 1904, it may also be the First tense. It is possible that *dyllo* may be in the same case, but I have no evidence.

First person plural :—*mar kefyn den,* "if we

find a man," D 647; *pan deffyn ny,* "when we come," R 773.

> These do not differ in form from the First tense, and we might be justified in looking upon the distinction of forms here as not going beyond the singular number. At the same time we have *mar kyf,* "if he finds," O 1103; *mar a's guel,* "if he sees you," D 1003; and many other instances, where there is a different form for the two tenses.

Second person plural:—*del y'm kyrreugh,* "as ye love me," O 543; *pan y'n guyllough,* "when you shall see him," R 1912.

Third person plural:—*mar a'n kefons,* "if they find him," D 582; *kyn teffons,* "though they come," R 392; *may teffons omma,* "that they come here," O 2408.

It is not unfrequent to find the vowel *a* or *e* suffixed to a verb in the second person singular in an interrogative or subjunctive construction; the following examples shew the practice:—

Interrogative.

prag ytheta, why goest thou? R 241.
pendra wreta, what doest thou? D 1185, 2981.
pendra vynta, what wilt thou? O 1311.
ple cleusta, where didst thou hear? O 2642.
pan a wrusta, what didst thou? D 2007.
a garsesta, wouldst thou love? D 2838.
a welte, seest thou? D 2925.
pendra ny vente, why wilt thou not? D 1775.
pe feste, where wast thou? O 467.
fattel thuthte, how didst thou come? R 260.
prag y tolste, why didst thou deceive? O 302.
a alsesta (galsesta), wouldst thou be able? R 862.

Subjunctive.

mar ny wreta, if thou dost not, R 1088.
na venta, that thou wilt not, D 1293.
pan leverta, since thou sayest, D 2017.

a'n guelesta, if thou shouldst see him, R 861.
mar a cruste (gruste) leverel, if thou didst say, D 1759.
aban golste, since thou hearkenedst, O 269.

In a few cases we find similarly the vowel *a* after a verb in the first person, and then the vowel is preceded by *m*; as, *pendra wrama*, what shall I do, R 679, D 856; *ellas pan fema gynys*, alas! that I was born! R 2207; *aban oma dasserghys*, since I am risen, R 2436; *hedre vyma ou pygy*, whilst I am praying, D 1013. See l. 1020.

I compare this to the addition of a vowel in such expressions as *ywe, ose, usy, wruge*, &c., where some kind of contingency or uncertainty is implied. We must for this suppose that the final *m*, as found in Irish, and in the oldest Welsh glosses, for the first person singular, is restored, as well as the *st* for the second person of the preterite, in *cleusta, feste*, as in the Welsh *ceraist*. In the second person of the First tense the dental yet remains, though weakened to *th*[a].

§. 27. Imperative. Second person: — *lavar*,

---

[a] I had supposed at first that *ma* and *ta* in these cases were the personal pronouns *my* and *ty* in an altered form; but the observation of an able philological friend has satisfied me that the explanation in the text is the true one. The grammatical value of the final vowel, when a verb follows certain conjunctions, such as *pan* or *mar*, is clear from the forms *gruge* and *duthe* instead of *gruk* and *duth* in O 423, D 524, and other passages. We are not bound to consider *ta*, in such words as *venta* and *leverta*, as necessarily additional to the verb; I look at *venta* and *leverta* as equivalent to *vennyth + a* and *leveryth + a* rather than to *venny + ta* and *levery + ta*; *wrama*, too, seems to be more probably *wram + a* than *wraf + ma*. There does not appear to be any reason for changing *my* and *ty* to *ma* and *ta*, whereas the annexation of *a* or *e* to a verb in a phrase denoting contingency is in accordance with the usage of the language.

"say," D 965; *treyl*, "turn," D 1155; *saf*, "stand," O 65.

Third person:—*guereses*, "let him help," O 2781; *gylwes*, "let him call," O 2774; *guyskyns*, "let him strike," D 2766; *tommans*, "let him warm," D 833.

First person plural:—*fystynyn*, "let us hasten," D 645; *leveryn*, "let us say," R 806; *guren*, "let us do," D 644.

Second person plural:—*levereugh*, "say ye," D 1109; *gueresough*, "help ye," D 1143.

Third person plural:—*kelmyns*, "let them tie," D 583.

§. 28. Infinitive:—*care*, "to love," O 1126, D 511; *leverel*, "to say," D 1759; *dybry*, "to eat," O 264; *danfon*, "to send," D 1615; *keusel*, "to speak," D 1276; *kyrhas*, "to fetch," O 2371; *myras*, O 1399, *myres*, O 1412, "to see."

Participle, active or present. Examples are numerous: the following are selected for the purpose of shewing the conversion of the sonant initial:—*ou corthye (gorthye)*, "worshipping," O 1616; *ou cul (gul)*, "making," O 1556; *ow kelwel (gelwel)*, "calling," O 2430; *ow querthe (guerthe)*, "selling," D 1520; *ou tos (dos)*, "coming," O 1651; *ou tysputye*, "disputing," D 1628. It is more like a neuter participle in *pan us gueyth ou tesehe*, "when the trees are drying," O 1128.

Participle, passive or past:—*kyrys*, "loved," R 892; *lythys*, "killed," R 903; *offrynnys*, "offered," O 1327; *gorrys*, "placed," R 430.

§. 29. Passives. First tense:—*aban na gefyr*

(*kefyr*) *ken*, "since no other is found," O 2503;
ple kefyr dyu grous aral, "where may two other
crosses be found," D 2576, compare *py kefer
pren*, D 2535; *del redyer in lyes le*, "as it is read
in many places," D 1168; *ma'n gueller a ver termyn*, "as will be seen in a short time," D 1940.

When the auxiliary verb is passive, the passive
sense is transferred to the principal verb:—

mar ny wrer (*gurer*) *y wythe*, if he be not guarded, R 341.
mar keller (*geller*) *y wythe*, if he can be kept, D 3058.
ny yllyr (*gyllyr*) *re the worthe*, thou canst not be too much
honoured, O 1852.

Third tense:—Zeuss, in p. 525, makes a passive
in *as* analogous to the old Welsh and Armoric *at*
(now *id.* W. and *ed*, Arm.). His examples are—
yn della y re thyskas, "thus they have been
taught," P. 80. 3, and *y torras* (printed *dorras*)
an veyn, "the stones were broken," P. 209. 4.
The old translators took this for the active third
person, and rendered the phrases given by "as
them others taught," and "they broke the stones;"
but an example from our book confirms the view of
Zeuss: *pan dorras queth an tempel*, "when the
vail of the temple was rent," D 3088: we may
perhaps cite also *fethas yu cas*, "the cause was
gained," R 579, and *uthyk yw clewas y lef*, "loud
was heard his voice," R 2340.

I have found very few instances of a passive verb used
in any other than the third person. In O 1 and D
873, we have *y'm gylwyr*, "I am called;" and in O
1924, *may haller agas cuthe*, "that you may be
covered:" see also O 1852, quoted above. These
are in accordance with Welsh; but it is difficult to
consider them precisely passives, because the pronoun, which ought to be the subject of the verb if
passive, is in the state especially employed when it is
the object. The view of Legonidec, the Breton gram-

marian, who calls these verbs Impersonals, and renders them by the pronoun *on,* as *on m'appelle,* appears the most suitable.

Fourth tense:—*ha re-na galser the rey,* "and those might have been given," D 537.

It may be as well to give a complete paradigm here, and the verb selected is *care,* "to love." The most regular forms are set down, but others will be found in the manuscript.

First tense:—' I love' or 'shall love.'

caraf, keryth, car : keryn, carough, carons.

Second tense:—'I was loving' or 'would love' or 'should love.'

caren, cares, care or *cara : caren, careugh, carens.*

Third tense:—' I loved.'

kerys, kersys, caras : kersyn, carsough, carsons or *carsans.*

Fourth tense:—' I had loved' or 'would have loved.'

carsen, carses, carse : carsen, carseugh, carsens.

Fifth tense:—' If I love.'

kyryf, kyry, caro : kyryn, kyreugh, carons.

Imperative:—' Love thou.'

car, cares or *carens : caren, careugh, carens.*

Infinitive:—*care,* "to love."

Participles:—*ou care,* "loving;" *kyrys,* "loved."

Passive, present and future: — *carer, keryr,* "is," or "shall be loved."

Conditional:—*carser,* "would be loved."

Past:—*caras,* "was loved."

VERBS.

As a general rule, whenever a question is asked, where there is not some interrogative pronoun or adverb, the letter *a* is put at the beginning; as, *a ny vynta obeye*, " wilt thou not obey ?" O 1505. Sometimes *a* is added when there is already an interrogative particle, probably to fill up the metre; as, *a pyth yu an keth deu-na*, " what is that same God ?" O 1485.

A negative is indicated by placing ny^2 or na^2 before a verb; as,

ny thue arte, it will not come again, O 1102.
na allaf sparie, that I cannot spare, O 946.
na wrello, that it may not do, O 1092.

Na is usually employed with imperatives and subjunctives.

§. 30. *Impersonal Conjugation.*

The Impersonal conjugation is generally employed when the nominative case precedes the verb directly, more especially when the nominative is a personal pronoun; the subject is generally followed by the particle *a*, and the initial of the verb takes the second form; the verb is always in the third person singular. This conjugation is so simple that it will be required merely to give a few examples of each case, to enable a student to understand it fully :—

me a lever, I say, R 1061.
me a sorras, I was angry, D 1421.
me a vynse (mynse), I would wish, D 211.
me re behas (pehas), I have sinned, O 249.
ty a wor (gor), thou wilt know, R 256.
ty a tew, thou wilt be silent, R 984.
ty a'n nahas, thou deniedst him, R 1351.
ty ru'm tullas, thou hast deceived me, O 252.
ty a'n guelse, thou wouldst have seen him, R 1382.

ef re gollas, he has lost, O 420.
ny a bys (*pys*), we pray, O 1072.
ny a dryg (*tryg*), we will remain, O 2112.
ny a gafas (*cafas*), we found, R 1474.
ny a'n recevas, we received him, R 2339.
ny a geusys (*keusys*), we spoke, R 1373.
why a gyf (*kyf*), you will find, D 176.
y a nyg, they fly, O 1068.
y a fyth (*byth*), they are, R 1477.

§. 31. *Compound Conjugation.*

The Compound conjugation is made by putting the auxiliary verb "to do" before the infinitive mood, as "I do love," "he does know," &c. in English. Sometimes *the* comes between the auxiliary and the infinitive. As this verb is irregular it is necessary to give the paradigm :—

TO DO.

Infinitive :—

gruthyl, D 198, O 1004; *guthyl*, O 1952; *guthul*, R 2252; or, *gul*, O 1174.

First tense :—

guraf, I do, O 1988.   *guren*, we do, O 1146.
gureth, thou dost, R 459.   *gureugh*, ye do, O 912.
gura, he does, 1376.   *gurons*, they do, D 2775.

We have *guregh*, D 814, for *gureugh*.

Second tense :—

gurellyn, I was doing, or, I would do, O 445.
gurelles, R 445 } thou wert doing or wouldst do.
gures, R 451
gure, R 6, D 1309 ⎫
gurefe, D 1316   ⎬ he was doing or would do.
gurella, D 1958   ⎪
gureva, D 2882   ⎭
gurellen we were doing or would do, O 183.
gurelleugh, ye were doing.
gurellens, they were doing.

VERBS. 59

Third tense :—

gurys (?) I did.
grussys, thou didst, O 222.
gruk, he did, R 158.
grussyn, we did.
grussough, R 40 ⎫
grussyugh, O 2792 ⎬ ye did.
grussons, they did, O 337.

When a conjunction comes before the third person singular, the form of the verb is generally *gruge*, a true subjunctive; as, *pan wruge*, O 423, 2250, D 913.

Fourth tense :—

grussen, I would have done, O 163.
grusses, thou wouldst have done, O 156.
grusse, he would have done, O 152.
grussyn, we would have done, R 2624.
grusseugh, ye would have done.
grussens, they would have done.

Fifth tense :—

guryllyf, that I may do, O 531.
gurylly, that thou mayst do, O 1784.
gurello, that he may do, R 498.
gurellen, that we may do, O 1048.
gurylleugh, that ye may do, D 811.
grons, that they may do, O 2034.

Imperative mood :—

. . . . *guren*, let us do, O 1170.
gura, do thou, D 1957. *greugh*, do ye, R 2232.
gurens, O 1093, ⎫
grens, D 371, ⎬ let him do. *gurens*, let them do.

Participle active :—

ou cul, doing, O 1556.

Participle passive :—

gurys, O 431, *gures*, done, O 988.

Passive :—

gurer, it is done, O 1936, R 341.

60   CORNISH GRAMMAR.

Note that *gu* in this verb is equivalent to *g* only: it does not make an additional syllable, and its mutations are those of *g*: we have thus *russe*, O 152, and *wrussen*, O 163.

The following example will suffice to shew the manner of using this conjugation :—

First tense :—

daggrow tyn guraf dyvere, bitter tears I shall shed, O 402.
an guel guraf the drehy, the rods I will cut, O 1988.
pan wreth agan dysky, when thou dost teach us, D 36.
an gorhel guren dyscuthy, the ark we will uncover, O 1146.
ny wreugh why tryge, ye shall not remain, O 317.
y wrons clamdere, they will faint, O 400.

Impersonal :—

y cuthe me a wra, cover him I will, D 1376.
my a ra y dybry, I will eat it, O 248.
hy a wra aspye, she will look, O 1115.
the verkye my a gura, mark thee I will, O 602.
ef a wra dynythy, he shall produce, O 638.
aga gora ty a wra, put them thou shalt, O 991.
goef a ra the serry, unhappy he who angers thee, O 1016.

This is the most ordinary way of making the future tense in Cornish.

Second tense :—

leverel gura na wrella dampnye, do say that he condemn not, D 1958.
na wrellen dybbry, that we should not eat, O 183.
an temple y wre terry, the temple he would destroy, D 1309.
y wrefe y threhevel, he would rebuild it, D 1316.

The conditional is generally made by this tense.

Third tense :—

pan wrussys cole, that thou didst hearken, O 222.
an sarf re ruk ow tholle, the serpent hath deceived me, O 286.

Imperative :—

gura ou gorthyby, answer me, O 301.

VERBS. 61

agan cuthe guren, let us cover ourselves, O 254.
greugh y tenne mes a'n dour, draw him out of the water, R 2232.

Infinitive:—

dre wul trogh, through breaking, O 298.

§. 32. *Passive Verb, made by the Verb substantive.*

It is much more usual to make up the passive verb by the verb substantive, as is done in most of the modern languages of Europe, than to use the passive inflection as explained in p. 45. For this purpose the paradigm of the verb substantive is required:—

Verb substantive.

The verb substantive in Cornish, as in other Indo-Germanic languages, has two roots; one of these appears to have been the letter *s*, and the other was the consonant *b*, interchanging with *f* and *w*. Examples of the first in Latin and English are *sum, es, est*, and *am, art, is*; of the second, *fui, fore*, and *be, was*. The Cornish, in some of its forms, has lost the initial *s*, but it regains the sibilant after *mar, nyn*, and some other words.

First division.

Present tense:—

of, I am, O 2049.	*on*, we are, O 2024.
os, thou art, R 1822.	*ough*, you are, R 196.
yu, he is, R 389.	*yns*, O 1691, *ens*, D 2353, } they are.

The third person singular is varied to *yw*, D 2952; *eu*, O 2214; *ew*, O 2572. All receive occasionally an addition at the beginning, becoming *assof, yssof, ythof, esof, sof, thof*, &c.; in the first three forms I see no difference in signification, and the additions in such cases are, I think, only variations of the verbal particles

CORNISH GRAMMAR.

a and *y*. Examples are, *asson whansek*, "we are desirous," D 37; *huhel ythos ysethys*, "high thou art seated," D 93; *yn ou colon asyw bern*, "in my heart is sorrow," D 2932; *yssyw hemma trueth bras*, "this is great sorrow," D 3182. I now believe that *esof*, *esos*, &c. are merely variations of these, though I have rendered them usually by the past tense: see D 931, 2511, R 1291. *Sof, sos, syu,* and *thof, thos, thyu,* &c. follow certain particles, as *mar, nyn,* &c.

There are some other forms for the present tense; *ma*, "is," scarcely differs from *yu*: see O 1316, 2561, 2633, R 2059. *Us* is like *ma*, but often implies 'who:' O 628, 1059, D 1410, 1425, R 2060; perhaps *eus* of R 316 may be the same word. We have *usy* in O 2692. *Yma* signifies 'there is,' O 410, 526, 775, R 400, 1216; *mons*, O 2091, and *ymons*, O 1687, 2084, are the plurals of *ma* and *yma*.

Imperfect tense :—

esen, I was, O 213.   *esen*, we were, R 1169, 2395.
eses, thou wast, O 900.   *esough*, ye were, D 332, R 2434.
ese, he was, O 1089.   *ens*, they were, D 2681, 2694 [a].

Preterite tense :—

o, "he was," O 706, 809, R 1096, 2007.

The forms *oma*, "I am," D 755; *osa*, D 1324, *ose*, D 1290, *oge*, O 1767, "thou art;" *ywe*, O 1822, *ugy*, R 1636, "he is;" and I think, *ony*, "we are," O 59; all these are either interrogative, or else they imply contingencies such as belong to the subjunctive mood.

Second division.

bones, O 2299, *bos*, D 2494, "to be."

First tense :—

bythaf, D 1932 } I shall be.
bethaf, O 2111 }

---

[a] I believe the real paradigm of the Present tense would be *of, os, yu: on, ough, yns;* and of the Imperfect, *en, es, e: en, eugh, ens;* but both tenses affected rather to lengthen

VERBS.

beþyth, O 1465
byþyth, O 1510 } thou shalt be.
byþ, he shall be, D 772.
beþyn, we shall be, O 1655.
byþeugh, you shall be, D 767.
beþens, O 2307
byþons, D 3093 } they shall be.

As there is a present tense in the first division, this tense is always, I think, future.

Second tense :—

bef, I should be, &c., O 2193.
bes, thou shouldst be, R 2442.
beþe, O 232
byþe, D 1948 } he should be.
ben, we should be, R 2423.
beugh, ye should be, D 5, 28.
bens, they should be, D 852.

The forms as well as the signification of this tense are confounded with those of the Fifth tense, and even of the Fourth. I cannot satisfy myself with any division of them.

Third tense :—

buf, *buef*, I was, R 1540, 2150.
bus, thou wast, D 1999.
bue, O 880, R 1443
be, O 2657, D 1154 } he was.
buen, we were, O 709, R 1823.
beugh, *bugh*, you were, R 192, 2243.
bons, they were, D 521.

Fourth tense :—

byen, I should be, O 2120, R 1942.
byes, thou shouldst be, D 2683.
bye, he should be, D 846, 1592.
byen, we should be,

their forms in actual use. In a similar way the Greeks added a syllable to the shorter forms of their verb substantive, writing εἶσθα and ἦσθα for εἶς and ἦς. Perhaps the Latin *esto* and *estote* originated in a like principle.

64 CORNISH GRAMMAR.

byeugh, ye should be, O 177.
byens, they should be.

> The forms *gyfye*, "would take," R 966, and *thothye*, "will" or "would go," R 2450, seem to be imitations of this tense.

Fifth tense :—

byf, beyf, I may or shall be, D 847, 2008.
by, thou mayst be, O 245, 2203.
bo, O 42, R 90 } he may or shall be.
be, O 396, 1112
ben, been, beyn, we may be, D 41, O 1973, 2699.
beugh, you may be, D 627.
bons, they may be, D 844, 899, 1546.

> The same observation as is made above at the close of the first division will apply here, in regard to the forms *byma*, D 1013, *befe*, O 2220, *befa*, D 905, *beva*, D 690, *bova*, D 620, *buve*, O 864, *bythe*, O 1327, *byse*, D 2908; and some others. Perhaps such additions are sometimes made merely to fill up a verse, as in *bosa* for *bos*, D 1120.

Imperative :—

byth, be thou, O 1341, 2616.
bethens, D 2374 } let him be.
bythens, D 794
bethon, let us be,
bethough, be ye, D 879.
bethens, let them be,

> Throughout the second division of this verb I have made the initial *b ;* but it occurs in the manuscript much more frequently written with a *v* or *f* from the influence of particles requiring a mutation, and frequently where I see no reason for such change; unless it be that a particle is implied though not expressed, as it is, I believe, the case in Welsh.

Examples of the passive verb made by help of the verb substantive :—

a'n nef of danfenys, from heaven I am sent, O 1372.
yth os ysethys, thou art seated, D 93.
yu gorhemmynnys thy'n, it is commanded to us, O 1049.

VERBS. 65

buthys on ny, we are drowned, O 1705.
yns plynsys, they are planted, O 2092.
bethaf lethys, I shall be killed, O 596.
ny fythyth sylwys, thou shalt not be saved, O 1510.
y fethons gorrys, they shall be put, O 342.
guynys may fuef, where I was pierced, R 1540.
helhys warbarth a fuen, we were driven together, O 709.
y fyen lethys, I should be killed, O 2120.
may fen guythys, that we may be preserved, D 41.
bos desesys, to be hurt, D 97.
bos rewardyys, to be rewarded, O 2201.

§. 33. A reflected verb is made, as in Welsh, by prefixing the syllable *ym*² (*em, om*). The equivalent in Armoric is *en em*.

Examples are frequent :—*ymwanas*, "he stabbed himself," R 2065, from the root *guan*; *emwyskys*, "he smote himself," R 2067, root *guask*; *ym den*, "withdraw," O 1377, root *ten*; *ny yllons ymweres*, "cannot help themselves," O 1420, root *gueres*; *mar ny wreth ymamendye*, "if thou do not amend thyself," O 1526. *Embloth*, in O 1661, meaning "to fight," is probably from the verb *lathe*, "to kill," something like the French *se battre*; though we have *emlathe y honan*, "to kill himself," in R 2073, where the writer perhaps added the pronoun *y honan* to avoid the ambiguity which might arise from the use of *emlathe*, meaning "to fight;" as a Frenchman might say, *il s'est battu lui-même*, meaning "he has beaten himself," while he would say, *il s'est battu*, when he wished to be understood, "he fought."

§. 34. IRREGULAR VERBS.

There are in Cornish some verbs irregular, which are generally irregular in Welsh and Armoric also. In going through the translation, I have jotted down a good many words which were at the time doubtful, and out of them I have been able to form the following incomplete paradigms: they might perhaps be completed by Welsh and Breton analogy, and no doubt several additional forms may be found, if the Cornish books be read through for the purpose; but I had no intention of venturing on a Grammar when the work was begun, and have not been able to supply the deficiencies since. I have consequently only incomplete results to offer; but in the case of every word set down, one passage at least is cited in which it occurs.

TO GIVE.

Ry, O 1801, 2606; *rey,* D 537.

First tense :—

rof, I give, R 857.   *ren,* (we give) D 2406.
reth, O 1814 }
reyth, D 472 } thou givest.
re, R 387, 674 }
ree or *rea,* O 2770 } he gives.

Second tense :—

ren, I would give (?) O 2739.

Third tense :—

res, D 2495 }
rys, O 320 } I gave.
ryssys, thou gavest, D 522.
ros, he gave, D 1384, R 165.   *rosons,* they gave, R 2601.

IRREGULAR VERBS. 67

Fifth tense :—
  rollo, that he may give, O 1823.
  rollons, that they may give, O 40.

Imperative :—
  ro, give thou, O 2010, R 83.
  roy, let him give, O 680, D 712.
  ren, let us give, D 1389.
  reugh, give ye, D 1362.

Participle present :—
  ou ry, giving, O 2316.

Participle past :—
  reys, given, D 1574.

TO BRING.

Dry, D 16, 273, 596.

First tense :—
  drow, D 3121 ⎫
  doro, D 1471 ⎭ I bring.

Second tense :—
  dregha, he would bring, R 403.

Third tense :—
  dros, he brought, O 111.

Fourth tense :—
  drosen, we would have brought, D 1976.

Imperative :—
  dro, O 1947 ⎫
  doro, O 1904 ⎭ bring thou.
  drens, let him bring, O 1933.
  dreugh, bring ye, O 1066, D 2329.

Participle past :—
  dreys, brought, D 2447, R 2328.

TO COME.

Dones, O 791; *dos,* R 570.

First tense:—

dueth, R 1178 } thou comest.
duth, R 882
due, it comes, D 2961, R 2273.
desons, they come, D 1247.

Second tense:—

dogha, that it may come, D 2912.

Third tense:—

duyth, D 2022 } I came.
dueyth, R 1661
duthys, R 2568 } thou camest.
dues, O 155
duth, R 2587 } he came.
dueth, R 234
dutheugh, ye came, R 193.

We have *aban duthe,* "since I came," D 517, 524, a subjunctive mood, as in *gruge:* see the verb *gruthyl* in p. 59.

Imperative:—

dus, O 2779 } come thou.
dues, R 308
dun, let us come, R 2305.
deugh, come ye, R 156, 1761.

Participle:—

des, come, D 352.

TO GO.

Mones, O 2030, D 232; *mos,* O 1603.

First tense:—

af, I go, O 339.

IRREGULAR VERBS.

eth, thou goest, O 2295, R 851.
a, he goes, R 2197.
en, we go, D 2997, R 2391.
eugh, ye go, O 2185.

Generally, *ythaf*, *ytheth*, &c.

Second tense :—

een, O 364
ellen, O 2193 } I should go.

Third tense :—

yth, I went, O 260, D 145.
etheugh, ye went, O 2086.

Fifth tense :—

ello, (when) he shall go, R 1563.

Imperative :—

ke, go thou, D 649.
eugh, go ye, R 179.
ens, let them go, D 173, R 2644.

TO BEAR or CARRY.

Don, D 2584, R 1226, 1241; *degy*, D 2313.

First tense :—

dek, R 2235, *deg*, O 903, 2814, he shall carry.

Third tense :—

dug, O 268, *duk*, O 2244, R 2554, he carried.

Fifth tense :—

dogo, that he may carry, R 2189.

Imperative :—

dok, D 1272, 2616
dog, O 1945, 2200 } carry thou.
doga, O 1298
degyns, let him carry, O 32, 1052, 1591.
degeugh, carry ye, O 2810, R 2184.

70   CORNISH GRAMMAR.

Participle present :—

ou toon, O 2820 } carrying.
ou ton, O 892

Past :—

degys, carried, O 1315.

TO KNOW.

gothfos, R 468; *gothfes*, R 195; *gothvos*, O 2098; *govos*, O 2102.

Present tense :—

gon, I know, R 1547.
gor, he knows, R 256.
gothough, ye know, R 2445.
gothons, they know, D 2774.

Future tense :—

gothfythy, thou shalt know, R 2381.
gothvyth, D 849 } he shall know.
govyth, O 188
gothfetheugh, ye shall know, R 1574.

These tenses are separated as in Welsh, where we have *gwn*, *gwr*, as a present tense, and *gwybydd*, *gwybyddwch*, as a future. They are analogous to the two divisions of the verb substantive.

Second tense :—

gothen, I did know, O 363.
gothes, D 848 } thou didst know.
gothas, D 2181
guythen, we did know, D 1914.

Fourth tense :—

gothfen, (if) we had known, R 2542.
gothfons, (if) they had known, D 2776.

Fifth tense :—

gothefaf, (if) I know, (?) R 719.
gothfo, (if) he know, O 190.

In *re woffe*, "may he know," O 530, we have the fifth, or second tense, converted into an imperative or optative by the verbal particle *re*. See p. 49. *Woffe* is = *gothfe*.

TO HAVE.

There is no verb in the Celtic language generally corresponding with the verb "to have;" in Cornish as in Welsh, the deficiency is sometimes supplied by *cafus*, "to take or find;" but the more usual substitute is like the Latin *est pro habeo*. We find thus *yma thy'mmo* (*est mihi*), "I have," D 494; *mar a'm be* (*si mihi fuerit*), "if I have," O 396; *na'm byth cres* (*non mihi est pax*), "I have no peace," R 1133. In most cases the verb is in the form *fyth*, the first tense of *bos*, as in *my a fyth, ty a fyth*, D 128, "I shall have, thou shalt have," &c. The Rev. R. Williams suggests that this may be "I possess," &c. from a root *meth*, the Welsh *meddu*; and this would be probable, the mutation of *m* and *b* being equally *f* or *v*; but the explanation will not suffice for the cases where the form is *byth*. I am inclined to think that the root is always *bos*;—that frequently the pronoun in the third form (§. 16. p. 27) was added to that in the first form, as in *why a's byth* (*vos vobis erit*), "you shall have," O 2586, D 3075, R 612, 672, *ny'm bes* (= *ny'm byth, non mihi est*), "I have not," O 171;—and that the sentiment of the real value of the word was sometimes lost, so that *ambyth* and *asbyth* were used like new verbs, as in *why asbetheyth*, "you shall have," D 33, and *ny ambyth*, "we shall have," O 1714. I suppose *ny'm bus*, R 1517, 2210, "I have not," to be a variant spelling of *ny'm byth;*—*na'm bes,* O 1884, to be the same, with a change of the negative;—and *a'mbues,* D 2392, to be *a'mbyth (mihi est);*—*as bues,* D 1970, and *agas bus,* R 2154, "you have," will be *a's byth. Am been,* "which I have," O 2613, and *ma'm vethen,* "that I may have," O 1958, are doubtful; *my a'n byth,* "I will have it," D 1187, may be read *vyth,* from *meth,* to possess;" the *v* and *b* are very much alike in the Manuscript. I cannot explain *ny gen byen ny,* "we should not have," of R 1029, except by reading *bye* for *byen.* A *bew* of D 2853, and *a's pew,* D 2855, 2858, are probably cognate with the Welsh *piau,* "to own;" as also *ty a bew,* "thou shalt have," O 974, which I have translated incorrectly. A *bywfy,* "which thou possessest," O 581, and *a bewe,* "which he possessed," O 2393, are probably from the same verb.

Another substitute for the verb "to have" is found in *ny's teve,* O 2597, D 508, *na's teve,* D 2647, *ny's tevyth,* O 300, 399, 1808, 1816, *a's tefo,* D 788, *a's tevyt,* O 2328. In all these I think the root is *tef* or *tev,* 'to grow' or 'come,' with the pronoun "her" or "them;" and that if the meaning were "he shall have," instead of "she or they shall have," we should find *a'n tefyth;* but this does not occur. In my note to O 2597, vol. I. p. 197, the conjecture about *ceve* appears wrong, and the version is far from literal: *tus,* meaning "men," is always considered grammatically as a feminine singular, and *s* of *ny's* agrees with it; I should therefore have rendered, "not have come to any man." The curious defective Armoric verb *devout,* "to have," is clearly analogous to that under consideration, and its forms *défé* and *deuz* or *devezo,* are related to *teve* and *tevyth.* See Legonidec's Grammar, p. 82.

ADVERBS, PREPOSITIONS, and CONJUNCTIONS.

The following list of Adverbs, Prepositions, and Conjunctions is incomplete, but it is hoped that it will be found useful; phrases from the Ordinalia, exemplifying the use of each particle, are added in every case.

§. 35. ADVERBS.

coul, cowal, quite.

    marrow cowal ty a vyth, killed quite thou shalt be, O 2702.
    bones an temple coul wrys, the temple to be quite done, O 2581.

kepar, " like, as," takes *ha* with a substantive, and *del* with a verb.

    kepar ha kuen, like dogs, R 172.
    kepar ha deu, like a god, O 290.
    kepar ha my, like me, O 2350.
    kepar del ve, as it was, O 872.
    kepar del vynny, as thou wilt, O 1046.

But we find

    kepar hag on, as we are, O 894.
    kepar ha me a welas, as I saw, R 1076.

and in one case,

    kepar ha del leverys, as I said, D 2690.

fattel², fatel, fettel, fettyl, how.

    fattel duthys yn ban, how didst thou come up? R 2568.
    ny won fatel yl wharfos, I know not how it can be, R 229.
    fettel allaf vy crygy, how can I believe? R 1423.
    prederys peb fettyl allo gorfenne, let all think how it can end, O 228.

prak, prag, pragh, why.

    prak y wreta thymmo amme, why dost thou kiss me? D 1105.
    prak y's guyskyth, why dost thou wear it? R 2549.

pragh yṭh hembrenkygh, why do ye lead? D 204.
prag yṭh yu ṭhe ṭhyllas ruṭh, why are thy garments red?
R 2567.

*maga*², *maga*⁰, as.

maga whyn (guyn) avel an leth, as white as the milk,
D 3138.
maga tek byṭhqueth del fue, as fair as ever he was, R 1659.
maga ta, "as well," is used in the sense of "also,"
as in English:—
den ha best magata, man and beast also, O 995.
ha war ṭhe treys magata, and on thy feet also, D 488.

namna, almost.

namnag of pur ṭhal, I am almost quite blind, O 1056.
namna'n dallas, almost blinded us, R 42.

ken, else.

ken ef a wra ou shyndye, else he will spit at me, O 2133.
bo ken deaul yw, or else he is a devil, R 2104.
When the sentence is negative, we find *nahen* (*na ken*),
although the negation be otherwise expressed; as
nahen na grys, think not otherwise, R 2038. See
also R 1126.

ot, ota, otte, wetta, welte, see, behold.

ot omma meneṭh huhel, see here a high mountain, D 125.
ot omme an guas, see here the fellow, R 1803.
ota saw bos, see the load of food, O 1053.
otte ṭhe vam, behold thy mother, D 2928.
ow ottoma ᵃ, see with me (?) R 2177.
a wetta ny, dost thou see us? D 2050.
a welte ṭhe flogh, seest thou thy son? D 2925.
The occurrence of these last forms shews the derivation
from the verb.

yn weṭh, yn weyṭh, also.

ha nef yn weṭh, and heaven also, D 290.
map deu os ha den yn weyṭh, son of God thou art and man
likewise, D 278.

ᵃ See the note to O 882, in p. 207 of the Ordinalia, vol. II.

ADVERBS.

tesen, perhaps.

 yn ur-na martesen, in that hour perhaps, D 2870.
 See the note to this passage in p. 213, vol. II. Ordinalia.

bytegyns, bytygyns, nevertheless.

 saw bytygyns cresough why, but nevertheless believe ye, R 1300.
 saw bytegyns ragon ny, but nevertheless for us, R 980. See also R 1016.

re², too much.

 thotho byny vye re, for him never would it be too much, R 2056.
 re hyr, too long, O 2548.
 re got (cot), too short, O 2549.

moghya, moghye, moghe, most.

 neb may fe moghya geffys, he who is forgiven most, D 513. See D 510, 514.

ketella, kettella, so.

 nep a rella yn ketella, whoever has done so, O 2240.
 yn kettella ny a vyn, so we will, D 243.

mar², so.

 mar tha (da), so good, O 912.
 mar ger (ker), so dear, O 612.
 pe feste mar bel (pel), where hast thou been so long, O 477.

pur², very.

 pur tha (da), very good, O 2572.
 pur thal (dal), very blind, O 1056.
 pur wyr (guyr), very true, R 1004.

bras, very, used after the adjective.

 del yu ef gallosek bras, as he is very powerful, O 1494.
 the colon yw cales bras, thy heart is very hard, O 1525.

fest, very, also after the adjective.

 wolcum fest, very welcome, D 1207.
 yeyn fest yu an awel, very cold is the weather, D 1209.

CORNISH GRAMMAR.

Adverbs of place.

omma, omme, umma, here.

> *fatel thuthevgh why omma,* how did ye come here, R 193.
> *ot omme an guas,* see here the fellow, R 1803.
> *Adam ottensy umma,* Adam, behold her here, O 102.

ena, eno, there.

> *ena yn dour,* there in the water, R 2196.
> *eno ny a'n recevas,* there we received him, R 2339.

ple (=pa le), where.

> *ny won ple fe,* I know not where it may be, O 1112.
> *ple me,* where is it? R 46.

a ves, outside.
agy, inside.

> *ares hag agy,* without and within, O 953.

> *Mes (ves),* the Welsh *maes,* forms also the following adverbs:—

the ves, away.
yn mes, out.

> *gallas an glaw the ves,* the rain is gone away, O 1097.
> *da yu yn mes dyllo bran,* it is good to send out a crow, O 1099.

alena, alene, thence.
alemma, hence.

> These adverbs are really phrases meaning "from that place," and "from this place," and I have often so divided them, though they are not distinguished in that way in the Manuscript. See R 2138, D 649, O 1945.

aber, aberth, aberveth, berth, within.

> *th'y worre aber yn beth,* to put him within the grave R 2108.
> *aberth yn beyth,* within the grave, R 2083.
> *dun aberveth,* let us come inside, O 1062.
> *berth yn bys-ma,* within this world, R 860.

ADVERBS.

adro, around.

> *tra ny vyth yn pow adro,* there is not a thing in the country round, O 189.
> *a'n beis ol adro,* of the world all around, O 404.

adrus, adrues, athwart, across, against.

> *adrus musury,* measure athwart, O 393.
> *tresters ty a pyn adrus,* beams thou shalt nail across, O 964.
> *kyn whrylly cous adrues,* though thou do speak against it, R 1792.

a hys, a heys, along.

> *groweth a hys,* lie at length, O 653.
> *groweth a heys,* lie along, O 1334.

oges, near.

> *na mos oges the'n wethen,* nor go near to the tree, O 184.
> *na nyl oges nag yn pel,* not one near nor at a distance, O 1141.

pel, far.

> *yma moyses pel gyllys,* Moses is far gone, O 1682.

a rag, in front.

> *war an brest a rag,* on the breast in front, O 2717.

yn rag, forward, forth.

> *deugh yn rag ketep onan,* come forward every one, O 2683.
> *dus yn rag,* come forth, O 2403.

yn kergh, on, away.

> *ke yn kergh dywhans,* go away quickly, R 116.
> *a'n beth yn kergh gyllys,* gone away from the tomb, R 809.

yn ban, up.

> *bynytha na thue yn ban,* he will never come up, R 2139.
> *Adam saf yn ban,* Adam, stand up, O 65.

Adverbs of time.

ytho, now, then.

> *ytho pyth yu the cusyl*, now what is thy advice? R 25.
> *ytho thy'm lavar*, now tell me, R 787.
> *ytho thy'nny yth hevel*, then to us it appears, D 1489.

> This appears to be rather the conjunction equivalent to the French *or*, than the true adverb of time: as in the Scripture phrase, "Now it came to pass." I am not quite sure that this is not the case often with the following also.

lemyn, lemmyn, lemman, now.

> *lemmyn a abesteleth*, now, O apostles! R 893.
> *lemyn sur yth yu eun hys*, now, surely it is the right length, O 2525.
> *lemyn ef yu agan guas*, now he is our fellow, O 910.
> *lemman warbarth ow fleghys*, now together, my children, D 307.

yn tor-ma, in this time, now.

> *na vo marow yn tor-ma*, that he be not killed now, D 2446.

agensow, agynsow, lately, just now.

> *me a'n guelas agynsow*, I saw him recently, R 896.
> *agensow my a'n guelas*, I saw him recently, R 911.

avar, early.

dewethes, late.

> *ha dewethes hag avar*, both late and early, O 629.
> *ha deug avar*, and come early, D 3239.

bynary, benary, for ever.

> *yn pouvotter venary*, in trouble for ever, O 898.
> *ny'th ty nahaf bynary*, I will not deny thee ever, D 907.

bynytha, never more.

> *bynytha ny thue yn bon*, never will he come up, R 2139.
> *my ny vennaf growethe bynytha*, I will never more lie down, O 625.

ADVERBS.

nefre, neffre, ever.

> *nefre y fyth acey,* ever shall be enmity, O 314.
> *nefre thyso re bo,* ever be it on thee, O 461.
> *the gous a bref neffre,* thy speech proves ever, D 1408.

avorow, to-morrow.

> *gueytyeugh bones avorow,* take care to be to-morrow, O 2299.
> *deug avar avorow,* come early to-morrow, D 3240.

hythew, hythew, to-day.

> *na moy cous thy'm hythew,* no more talk to me to-day, R 1940.
> *wheth bys hythew,* yet till to-day, R 1550.

athesempys, dyssempys, &c., immediately.

> *athysempys thu'm tage,* immediately to choak me, D 1528.

toth, touth, haste.

> This word appears to be a noun, used in combination adverbially.
> *ow treyle thotho touth da,* turning from him speedily, (i. e. good haste) D 558.
> *heeth ou bool touth ta,* reach my axe quickly, O 1001.
> *tho'm gurek ka'm flehes totta,* to my wife and children speedily, O 1036. (Totta = toth ta.)
> *cowyth dun toth da,* companion, let us come quickly, D 643.
>> In D 660 we have *gans touth bras,* "with great haste." shewing that the word is a substantive; and in D 662 *toth men,* of the same meaning, but which I do not understand.

kettoth, ketoth, as soon as.

> *kettoth an ger,* as soon as the word, O 1908.
> *kettoth ha'n ger,* as soon as the word, R 1970.
> *ketoth ha'n ger,* as soon as the word, O 2272.

arte, again.

> *gorryn ef yn beth arte,* let us put him into the grave again, R 2100.
> *ny'm guelyth arte,* thou shalt not see me again, O 244.

80 CORNISH GRAMMAR.

solaṭhyṭh, solabrys, some time ago.
> I find this compound adverb half a dozen times; the root is clearly *sol,* and the addition is *prys,* "time," or *dyṭh,* "day." See *solabrys,* O 2322; *solabreys,* O 2747; *sollabreys,* D 746; *solaṭhyṭh,* O 2612; *solaṭheṭh,* R 1929, and *sollaṭhyṭh,* R 2380.

kyns, before.
> *teke ages kyns y van,* fairer than it stood before, D 348.
> *y fue kyns y vos gurys,* there were, before it was done, D 350.

warlergh, afterwards.
> *sau me warlergh drehevel,* but I, risen afterwards, D 896.

whare, wharre, soon.
> *ha whare a,* and will soon go, O 642.
> *may tewe an tan wharre,* that the fire may light soon, D 1221.

yn makes an adverb of a substantive or adjective; sometimes it is yn^2, sometimes yn^o, and sometimes no change is made.
> *yn sur,* surely, R 529.
> *yn teffry,* really, R 565.
> *yn pur deffry,* very really, D 300.
> *yn tyen,* entirely, O 2589.
> *yn guyr,* truly, O 2541.
> *yn len,* faithfully, O 2608.
> *yn ta,* well, O 2523.
> *ṭhe ierusalem yn fen,* to Jerusalem quite, O 1948.
> *yn fen guren ny,* quite let us do, R 1242.
> [*yn fen* = to the end.]
> *yn felen,* as a felon, O 2653.
> *yn kettep guas,* every fellow, D 1350.

---

§. 36. PREPOSITIONS.

a^2, of or from. (See §. 17, p. 31.)
> *luen a byte* (*pyte*), full of pity, O 2369.
> *a pup squythens y sawye,* from all weariness cure him, D 477.
> *terrys ol a'y le,* broken all from its place, D 356.

PREPOSITIONS.

adre, adres, adro, around.

    adres pow, around the country, R 1477.
    adre thethe, around them, O 2097.
    adro thotho, around it, O 2101.
    adro thethy, around it (feminine), O 778.

agy, agey, within; (followed by *the.*)

    agy the lyst, in the lists, R 223.
    agy the ewhe an geyth, within the evening of the day, R 275.
    agey the'n cyte, within the city, D 627.

athyworth, thyworth, theworth, from.

    kyns denas athyworto, before withdrawing from it, O 1401.
    my a's pren thyworthys, I will buy it of thee, D 1555.
    thyworth ow pen, from my head, D 1145.
    theworth urry re thuk, hast taken from Uriah, O 2244.

athyrag, in presence of.

    athyragough me a pys, before you I pray, D 1414.
    athyragof my re weles, I have seen before me, O 1955.

a-ugh, over.

    nyg a-ugh lues pow, fly over many countries, O 1136.
    the tacky'e a-ugh y pen, to fasten it over his head, D 2808.

avel, as, like.

    avel gos, like blood, R 2500.
    avel dewow, like gods, O 178.
    avel servont, like a servant, D 804.

awos, notwithstanding, because of.

    awos ol ow gallos, notwithstanding all my power, D 53.
    awos the theu na'y vestry, notwithstanding thy god and his power, O 2738.
    ny yl bos awos an beys, it cannot be for the world, R 2471.
    awos deu, for God's sake, O 2564.

bys, as far as.

    bys yn ierusalem ke, unto Jerusalem go, O 1928.
    bys yn y chy, even to his house, D 648.
    bys deth fyn, till the last day, D 724.

dan, under.

> *yn dan gen*, under the chin, O 2712.
> *a than the glok*, from under thy cloak, D 2682.
> *yn dan an chek*, under the kettle, R 139.

dre, for, by, through. (See §. 17, p. 31.)

> *hy a'n gruk dre kerense*, she did it for love, D 549.
> *dre ow fynys*, through my pains, D 45.
> *dre un venen wharvethys*, wrought by a woman, O 620.
> *kentrow dre ow thrys*, nails through my feet, R 2587.

dres, dreys, over, beyond.

> *dres dyfen ou arluth ker*, beyond the prohibition of my dear Lord, O 172.
> *ow mos dres pow*, going over the country, R 1511.
> *dreys dour tyber*, through the river Tiber, R 2214.

er, by.

> *er an treys*, by the feet, R 2082.
> *er the fyth*, on thy faith, O 1441.
> *er an thewen*, by the gods, O 2651.
>
> *Er* appears to be identical with *or* and *war*; see note to D 202, vol. I. p. 236.

erbyn, against, towards. (Lat. *obviam*.)

> *erbyn a laha*, against law, D 572.
> *erbyn haf*, against summer, O 31.
>
> *Erbyn*, with a pronoun, receives the pronoun between *er* and *byn*, making the usual mutations; as *er ow fyn*, R 2573; *er y byn*, D 235. See §. 11. p. 18.

gans, with, (accompanying.) (See §. 17, p. 31.)

> *gans ow tas*, with my father, D 727.
> *lanters gans golow*, lanterns with light, D 609.

gans, by, with, (instrument, manner, cause, agency.)

> *gans ow deu lagas me a wel*, with my eyes I see, D 410.
> *gans myyn gureugh hy knoukye*, with stones strike her, O 2694.
>
> *gans peder ha iowan parys*, by Peter and John prepared, D 700.
> *gans touth bras*, with great speed, D 660.

PREPOSITIONS.

hep².
> *y a tremyn hep thanger*, they shall pass without danger, O 1615.
> *hep thout*, without doubt, O 2668.
> *hep worfen*, without end, D 1562.

herwyth, herweth, according to.
> *herwyth y volungeth ef*, according to his will, O 1320.
> *herweth the grath*, according to thy grace, O 2253.

kyns², before.
> *kyns pen try dyth*, before the end of three days, D 347.
> *kyns vyttyn*, before morning, O 1644.

lemmyn, except.
> *nag ens deu byth lemmyn ef*, there are no gods except him, R 1751.

marnas, except.
> *war pep ol marnas ty*, over all but thee, O 948.

mes, yn mes, out of.
> *greugh y tenne mes a'n dour*, drag him out of the water, R 2232.
> *tynneugh yn mes agan temple*, drag out of our temple, O 2693.
> *mar seugh mes a dre*, if you go from home, O 2185.

rag, rak, for, because of. (See §. 17, p. 30.)
> *rak eun kerenge*, for real love, D 483.
> *rak ow anclythyas*, for my burial, D 548.
> *rak the servys*, for thy service, D 613.
> *teweugh rak meth*, silence for shame, R 1495.
> *yw ou colon trogh rag agas cous*, my heart is broken because of your talk, R 1365.
> *rag the offryn ker*, because of thy dear offering, O 567.

rag, from.
> *guythys rak an bylen*, preserved from the evil one, D 41.
> *guyth vy rak an ioul*, preserve me from the devil, R 1564.
> *guythe ef rag tarofvan*, preserve it from fantoms, O 2364.

a rak, before, in presence of.
> *a rak pilat*, before Pilate, R 2593.
> *a rak agan lagasow*, before our eyes, R 1492.

re, by, (swearing.)

> *re iovyn,* by Jove, O 1532.
> *re synt iovyn,* by Saint Jove, R 349.
> *re deu an tas,* by God the Father, O 1919.

ryp, beside, near.

> *ryp ihesu cryst gorrys,* put beside Jesus Christ, R 266.
> *me a gosk ryp y pen,* I will sleep by his head, R 418.
>> In the line *yn plas us omma rybon,* D 460, we have clearly the preposition *ryp* joined to the pronoun of the 1st pers. plural: *rybon,* "beside us."

saw, except, without.

> *saw y ober ha'y thyskes,* without his work and his teaching, D 57.
> *ny hynwys thy'm saw pedar,* he named none to me except Peter, R 916.

tan, by.

> *tan ou feth,* on my faith, O 2534.
> (Not found elsewhere.)

the, to. (See §. 17, p. 31.)

thyworth, theworth, from.   See *athyworth.*

trogha, troha, towards.

> *stop an wethen trogha'n dor,* bend the tree towards the ground, O 201.
> *fystyn trogha parathys,* hasten towards Paradise, O 332.
> *troha ken pow,* towards another country, O 344.
> *fystynyugh troha'n daras,* hasten towards the door, O 349.

war², upon. (See §. 17, p. 31.)

> *war veneth (meneth),* upon a mountain, O 1281.
> *war beyn (peyn) cregy,* on pain of hanging, O 2280.
> *war thu (du),* to God, D 40, 357.
> *war tyr veneges,* on blessed ground, O 1407.

warlergh, after, according to, (receives a governed pronoun in the middle, like *erbyn.*)

> *warlergh the gussullyow,* after thy counsels, O 2269.
> *war the lergh owth ynwethe,* craving after thee, R 1170.
> *war aga lergh fystynyn,* after them let us hasten, O 1641.

worth, at, to, against. (See §. 17, p. 32.)

    ṭhe tros worth men, thy foot against a stone, D 98.
    worth an treytor, to the traitor, D 1449.

wose, woge, after.

    syṭhyn wose hemma, a week after this, O 1026.
    woge soper, after supper, D 834.

wos°. (Not found elsewhere.)

    wostalleth na wosteweṭh, at first, nor at last, O 2762.

        This may be equivalent to *war + dalleth*, and *war + deweṭh*; compare *wor tyweṭh*, D 1818.

yn, in, into. (See §. 17, p. 30.)

    nyn sa yn agas ganow, it goes not into your mouth, O 1913.
    yn ou enef, in my soul, D 1022.
    yn pup termyn, at all times, D 1040.

yntre, ynter, among, between.

    yntre y ṭhyns (dyns) ha'y davas (tavas), between his teeth and his tongue, O 826.
    yntre an mor ha'n tyryow, between the sea and the lands, O 26.

        yntre and *ynter* take *ṭh* before a pronoun, like the prepositions enumerated in §. 17.

    yntreṭho ha'y gowethe, between him and his companions, D 1288.
    yntreṭhe gasaf ow ras, among them I leave my grace, R 1584.
    yntreṭhon, between us, O 936.
    ol cres yntreṭhough, all peace among you, R 2433.
    me a ṭhybarth ynterṭhogh, I will divide between ye, D 2325.

§. 37. CONJUNCTIONS.

aban, since, because.
>*aban ywe yn della*, since it is so, D 1953.
>*aban golste worty hy*, because thou hearkenedst to her, O 269.
>*aban na vynta cresy*, since thou wilt not believe, O 241.

ages, es, ys, eys, than.
>*teke ayes kyns*, fairer than before, D 348.
>*tekke alter es del us genen*, a fairer altar than such as is with us, O 1179.
>*gueth ys ky*, worse than a dog, R 2026.
>*hacre mernans eys emlathe*, a more cruel death than self-killing, R 2073.

>>*Es* and *ages* take suffixed pronouns, as do the prepositions enumerated in §. 17.

>*ken deu agesos*, another God than thou, R 2477.
>*ken arluth agesso ef*, another Lord than him, O 1789.
>*y fynnaf vy mos pella esough*, I will go further than you, R 1299.
>*ken agesough*, other than you, O 2357.

bo, or.
>*bo ken deaul yw*, or else he is a devil, R 2104.

drefen, because.
>*drefen na fynnyth crygy*, because thou wilt not believe, R 1106.
>*drefen un wyth the henwel*, because of once calling on thee, O 2724.

erna, until.
>*erna wrello tremene*, until she be dead, O 2695.
>*erna'n prenny*, until thou pay for it, O 2653.

ha, and.
>*map ha tas*, Son and Father, D 297.
>*ov tus hammy (ha my)*, my people and me, O 971.

>>Takes *g* before a vowel, as, *hag yn tyr*, and in the earth, O 27; *hag ef ha kemmys*, both he and as many as, R 1760.

CONJUNCTIONS.

hedre, whilst, as long as.

> *hedre vyyn ou predery*, whilst I am considering, O 2035.
> *hedre veyn beu*, as long as I am living, D 115.
> *hedre vy may fo anken*, until it be that death is, O 276.
> *hedre ro yn the herwyth*, as long as it is in thy power, O 1464.
> *hedre vyugh byu*, as long as ye are living, O 2349.
> *hedre vyns y yn ou gulas*, as long as they shall be in my kingdom, O 1503.

kyn, ken, though.

> *kyn fe terrys*, though it be broken, D 354.
> *ken nag of guyw*, though I am not worthy, D 481.
> *kyn wrello son*, though he should make a noise, R 2016.

kettel, when.

> *kettel tersys an bara*, when thou didst break the bread, R 1318.
> *kettel thueth er agan pyn*, when he came to meet us, R 1329.

lemmyn, but.

> *nyn syu gulan lemmyn mostys*, it is not clean but dirty, R 1927.
> *lemmyn yn tan bos cuthys*, but in fire to be covered, R 2326.

ma, that.

> *pys e ma'n danfonno*, pray him that he send him, R 1620.
> *ma na wothfo gorthyby*, that he may not know how to reply, D 1660.
> *ma gas bo*, that it be to you (that you may have), D 226.

*mar*ᵃ, *mara*°, if.

> *mar qureugh (gureugh) ou wylas*, if ye do seek me, D 1121.
> *mar a'n pesaf ef*, if I pray him, D 1166.
> *mara keusys falsury*, if I spoke falsehood, D 1271.
> *mara pethe (bethe) lel iuggys*, if he be fairly judged, D 1344.
> *mara qureta (gureta)*, if thou dost, D 1385.
>
>> Before the verb substantive, and some others with an initial vowel, *mar* takes *s* or *th*, which apparently had nearly the same sound; (see §. 4. p. 8); as *mar syu*, "if he is," R 520; *mar sos*, "if thou art," D 60; *mar seth*, "if thou go," O 2652; *mar seugh*, "if you go," O 2185; *mar thes*, "if thou be," O 608. *Mara*

is frequently used in this case: *mara syw*, "if it be," O 2563, R 828; *mara sethe*, "if he be gone," R 538. The Manuscript is not constant in dividing the words, and I have also been very uncertain about it in the text: I should now be inclined to join the *s* or *th* to the verb, considering it, in the verb-substantive at least, to be a restoration of the original sibilant. See p. 93.

Perhaps we should always write *mar a* divided; the division is complete in R 2542, two words intervening: *mar fur torment a cothfen*, "if we had known the cruel torment."

marnes, mars, unless.

marnes drethos vernona, unless by thee Veronica, R 2220.
mars dre mur our, unless by much gold, R 1964.
mars cryst a weres, unless Christ helps, R 2132.
mas in R 47 and O 1504 may be put for *mars*.

may, that.

may tewe an tan wharre, that the fire may kindle soon, D 1221.

mes, but.

mes mara keusys yn lel, but if I have spoken truly, D 1273.

*pan*², when, since.

han vyrwyf (myrwyf), when I die, D 227.
pan cam worthybys, when he answered rudely, D 1403.
pan theugh mar freth, when you come so bold, D 1115.ᵃ

Pan appears to be used also in the way of deprecation, as,

govy pan y'n gruga, wo is me that I did it! D 1434.
ellas vyth pan ruk cole, alas! that I ever listened, O 626.

rag, rak, ragh, for, because.

rag pur tha ew, for it is very good, O 2572.
ragh map an pla, for the son of evil, D 10.
rak the vones dycythys, for that thou art come, D 280.

py, or.

pynak vo lettrys py lek, whether he be lettered or lay, D 681.

ᵃ This is probably a present tense of the verb *dones,* 'to come.'

yn nep bos tewl py yn sorn, in some bush, hole, or in a corner, R 539.
nep a serf py a theber, he who serves, or who eats, D 799.

sau, saw, but.

sau dystogh hy a ryth due, but soon it will be done, O 2178.
sau an ethyn byneges, but the blessed birds, O 1067.
saw bytegyns ragon ny, but nevertheless for us, R 980.

§. 38. CONSTRUCTION.

The few observations collected while making the version of the Dramas are too desultory to admit of the name of Syntax; much of what might pass under that name is incorporated with the preceding pages, and the few remaining observations are set down here without much pretension to system. It may be observed once for all, that the exigencies of metre have apparently compelled the author of these Dramatic Writings to such inversions and irregularities as are met with in all earlier attempts at metrical composition.

When a transitive verb governs an accusative substantive, the pronoun corresponding with the substantive is often added, as, *me a's ygor an darasow*, R 638, literally, "I will open them the doors;" *an mernans me a'n kymmer*, O 1332, "the death I will take it;" *ha henna ny a'n guylwyth*, R 53, "and that we shall see it;" *an gorhel my a'n gura*, O 966, "the ship I will make it."

When a verb which has a plural subject comes before the subject, it does not agree with it, but is put in the singular: as, *y fyth agan enefow*, "our souls shall be," D 75; *re'n kergho an dewolow*, "may the devils fetch him," R 2277.

CORNISH GRAMMAR.

When a verb in the infinitive mood follows a verb implying motion, it is commonly preceded by *the*, as in English by the corresponding particle "to:" as,

dun ny the veras, let us come to see, O 2325.
dun the gyrhas, let us come to fetch, O 2371.
mos the vyras, to go to see, D 1399.
eugh th'y drehy, go to cut it, O 2505.
deu a'm danfonas the wofyn, God sent me to ask, O 1431. But we have also *rag*, as in *dun rag offrynna*, "let us come to offer," O 1307. *Dun*, 'come,' in these cases is like the English 'come along.' where other languages use 'go.'

When the infinitive expresses the object or aim of a verb going before, it is preceded by *rag*, corresponding with the French *pour*, and our own vulgar "for:" as,

gorre an prynner rag lesky an sacryfys, put the wood (for) to burn the sacrifice, O 1324.
lafurye a wra rak dry den, he will labour to bring man, D 16.
ny a vyn mos rak y worthe, we will go to worship him, D 236.

After an auxiliary verb the infinitive comes immediately, without any preposition: as,

mar mynnyth hy dystrewy, if thou wilt destroy her, O 2675.
ny vennaf cafus le, I will not take less, D 594.
na allaf kerthes, nor can I go on, O 374.
ma yllyn mos, that we may go, D 708.

But we have also

mennaf the terry, I will break, D 485.

and sometimes there is no preposition where we should expect to find *the*; as,

me a'th pys agan sawye, I pray thee to save us, D 272.

Instead of using the conjunction "that" with another verb in the indicative mood, as in most European languages, it is usual to put the second verb in the infinitive preceded by the personal pronoun, as is common in Latin:

> *ha cous ef the thasserhy*, and say that he has risen, R 24.
> *marth a'm bues ty the lererel folneth*, it is a wonder to me that thou shouldst speak folly, R 961.
> *nyn sa y'm colon why the geusel*, it goes not into my heart, (i. e. I do not believe) that you have spoken, R 1481.
> *del won the bos*, as I know thee to be, R 859.

The subjunctive mood is used in its natural signification: that is to say, whenever the verb expresses an uncertainty, or expectation, or contingency of any sort, without regard to any conjunction preceding; thus Mary Magdalene says, *ken nag of guyw,* "though I am not worthy," D 481, in the indicative mood, acknowledging her own unworthiness; but the gaoler directs his servant to put Pilate in prison, *kyn wrello son,* "though he may make a noise," R 2016; and this notwithstanding both verbs are preceded by the same conjunction: the French language would use the subjunctive in both cases; *quoique je sois,* and *quoiqu'il fasse.* So *del os luen a ras,* "as thou art full of grace," O 106, in the indicative, expressing a full belief, and *del y'm kyrry,* "as thou lovest me," O 537, in the subjunctive, where a doubt is implied. This is however not always observed; the Cornish writers were hardly skilled enough in composition to be always accurately guided, and rhyme or metre was frequently exigent. The following examples of the subjunctive mood will suffice to give an insight into its use.

> *er na wrello tremene*, (beat her) until she be dead, O 2695.
> *er na'n prenny*, (thou shalt not get away) until thou pay for it, O 2653.
> *kyn fe an temple dyswrys,* though the temple were destroyed, D 365.

may hyllyf y lathe, (give me a sword) that I may kill him, R 1969.
pys e thy'm ma'n danfonno, pray him that he send him to me, R 1620.
ma na wothfo, that he shall not know, D 1660.
dre clethe nep a vewa, he who lives by the sword, D 1158.

NOTE.

Since the preceding sheets were printed, the following forms have been noticed in the irregular verbs:—

In p. 68. 1st tense,   *deugh*, ye come, D 1115.
                        dethons, they come, Pas. 258, 1.
        Imperative, *deug*, come ye, R 3239.
In p. 70. 2d tense,   *gothyen*, I knew, R 2544, 2559.
                        gothye, he knew, Pas. 101, 2.
                        ?*gotham*, Pas. 245. 3.
        4th tense, *gothfes*, thou knewest. O 151.
        5th tense, *gothfy*, thou shalt know, D 1042.
        Participle, *gothvethys*, known, O 1520.
In p. 63, apparently in the 4th tense of the verb substantive, *beyn*, D 115.
                        byyn, O 2035. qu. plural.
                        byugh, O 2349.
                        byns, O 1503.

The following forms of Irregular Verbs may be added to the preceding; they have been found since the others were printed.

dora, I should bring, R 1789.
drew, bring ye, D 178.
drewh, bring ye, R 1776.
druth, brought, R 2492.
druyth, brought, O 1621.
dres, brought, D 1569.
dues, to come, R 647.
deve, I come, R 2620.
de, will come, O 2431, D 541.
dy, will come, D 1654.
dufe, (if) he come, R 7.
den, let us come, O 2543.
deugh, ye come, D 1115.
duegh, come ye, R 323.
dens, let them come, D 694.
dothe, may come, O 1744.
dothye,? R 2450.
ow tos, coming, D 370, R 145.
eth, he went, 3rd tense, R 835.
ylly, thou shalt go, 5th tense, R 2452.
ou mos, going, R 2298.
gothyen, I knew, 2nd tense, R 2544, 2559.
gothyan, I knew, 2nd tense, R 2614.
gothfen, I should know, 4th tense, D 1287.
gothfye, he would know, 4th tense, D 490.
gothfough, ye should know, 4th tense, D 2156.
gother, the passive, O 2332.
guren, I would do, 2nd tense, D 1622, R 1894.
gurefa, he may do, 2nd tense, R 2473.

F

gurellough, you may do, 2nd tense, D 2196.
grussyn, we did, 3rd tense, R 1341.
gruga (that) I did, 3rd tense, D 1434.

When the present participle governs a pronoun, it is made by *orth* or *worth*, instead of *ou* or *ow* : as *ymons y orth y sywe*, they are following him, O 1688 ; *ythese gans Ihesu worth y servye*, he was with Jesus serving him, D 1406. See also D 342, 442, 1141, 1333, 2994.

Made in the USA
Middletown, DE
27 October 2023

41392993R00059